MW01078444

Start with Strips

13 Colorful Quilts from 2½" Strips

Susan Ache

Martingale®
Create with Confidence

Start with Strips: 13 Colorful Quilts from 2½" Strips
© 2017 by Susan Ache

Martingale®
19021 120th Ave. NE, Ste. 102
Bothell, WA 98011-9511 USA
ShopMartingale.com

No part of this product may be reproduced in any form, unless otherwise stated, in which case reproduction is limited to the use of the purchaser. The written instructions, photographs, designs, projects, and patterns are intended for the personal, noncommercial use of the retail purchaser and are under federal copyright laws; they are not to be reproduced by any electronic, mechanical, or other means, including informational storage or retrieval systems, for commercial use. Permission is granted to photocopy patterns for the personal use of the retail purchaser. Attention teachers: Martingale encourages you to use this book for teaching, subject to the restrictions stated above.

The information in this book is presented in good faith, but no warranty is given nor results guaranteed. Since Martingale has no control over choice of materials or procedures, the company assumes no responsibility for the use of this information.

Printed in China
22 21 20 19 18 17   8 7 6 5 4 3 2 1

Library of Congress Cataloging-in-Publication Data is available upon request.

ISBN: 978-1-60468-871-9

MISSION STATEMENT

We empower makers who use fabric and yarn
to make life more enjoyable.

CREDITS

**PUBLISHER AND
CHIEF VISIONARY OFFICER**
Jennifer Erbe Keltner

CONTENT DIRECTOR
Karen Costello Soltys

DESIGN MANAGER
Adrienne Smitke

MANAGING EDITOR
Tina Cook

PRODUCTION MANAGER
Regina Girard

ACQUISITIONS EDITOR
Karen M. Burns

**COVER AND
INTERIOR DESIGNER**
Kathy Kotomaimoce

TECHNICAL EDITOR
Elizabeth Beese

PHOTOGRAPHER
Brent Kane

COPY EDITOR
Melissa Bryan

ILLUSTRATOR
Lisa Lauch

SPECIAL THANKS
*Photos for this book were taken at Lori Clark's
The FarmHouse Cottage in Snohomish, Washington.*

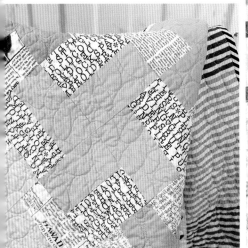

Contents

Introduction

I adore scrappy quilts, and the scrappier the better. I used to organize all of my scraps by size, but then I realized that I'm a color-oriented person. Now I organize my scraps by color, regardless of their size, and I enjoy the process much more.

I also like working with precuts (especially Jelly Rolls, which are sets of 2½"-wide fabric strips), because they make it easy to add a little bit of a lot of different fabrics to my quilts. As a scrap quilter, that really appeals to me. But I don't always love playing with just one complete line of fabric. So, just as with my scraps, I organize my precuts by color too. I can practically hear you saying, "What?!"

Yep, that means the minute I get a Jelly Roll home, I open up the roll, separate the strips, and divvy them up into the color bins where they belong. It's far easier for me to grab a color bin to jump-start my inspiration rather than to hunt through multiple bins for what I need.

As a result, you'll find that many of the quilts in this book aren't made from one or even two Jelly Rolls of the same fabric line. I love to use Jelly Roll strips, I just don't use them the way many people do. I mix them up to create my own variety of colors and prints—regardless of how they came packaged.

To learn more about how I work with precuts, read through the next section for some of my tips. Hopefully you'll find this way of working with precut strips a bit freeing and a whole lot of fun. Or jump right to the projects, pick your favorite, and then come back to my tips if you need some advice. Whichever way you choose to use this book, I hope you have fun sewing some of my favorite scrappy designs.

Susan

> "...I don't always love playing with just one complete line of fabric."

> "I love to use Jelly Roll strips, I just don't use them the way many people do. I mix them up to create my own variety..."

A New Way to Work with Precuts

Let's face it, we all love them. They're like quilters' candy sitting near the checkout counters at our favorite quilt shops. Who can resist a charm pack, Layer Cake, or Jelly Roll? They each offer at least one of every fabric in a fabric line, providing lots of options for those of us who like scrappy quilts. And they're planned to go together, so fear of combining fabrics is a thing of the past.

But, following a predetermined plan is not exactly how I like to work with precuts. I really do mix them up and sort them by colors, so when I want to make a quilt that's predominantly red and green, I can easily find all the red and green strips I own and be on my way. If that sounds intimidating, let me share some of my secrets that will make it easy.

Start with Charm Packs

Even though I made the quilts in this book using 2½" strips, I typically start by buying charm packs (precut stacks of 5" squares). They're my inspiration jumping-off point. I buy them just so I can see the prints in a line of fabrics. I keep these charm packs off to the side so that I can grab them and start a collage of sorts when it's time to plan a quilt. I store them with paint-color chips and any miscellaneous pictures I may have printed for color inspiration. Then, once I know which fabrics I like and which bundles they're from, I can purchase yardage or Jelly Rolls and get started.

"...following a predetermined plan is not exactly how I like to work with precuts."

Make Practice Blocks

If you're not sure what colors you want to use, or if you want to try out a new technique that will be called for in a particular project, do what I do and make practice blocks. This may sound funny, but I make all my practice blocks in solids. My go-to background for my practice blocks (and for my actual quilts) is an ivory solid—Bella Solids #60 from Moda, to be precise. You may not need to make a practice Nine Patch block, but whenever I'm trying out a block I've never made before, or when I'm testing a technique I'm not sure I'll love enough to repeat 20 times over, I make a practice block. Because I consider these experiments, I don't want to use the "real fabric." At some point in my life I will have a completely scrappy block quilt in nothing but solids!

"This may sound funny, but I make all my practice blocks in solids."

Ready for Jelly Rolls

Once I've determined that I like the new block design or technique, I'm ready to forge ahead with print fabrics. As I mentioned in my introduction, I sort all my fabric scraps by color. That goes for Jelly Rolls, too. That way, when I want to make a scrappy quilt with a limited color palette, I can find all of the orange or green or turquoise strips I need, without having to thumb through individually bundled Jelly Rolls.

As you'll see in the project instructions, I sometimes call for a certain number of strips of each color. That doesn't mean they all have to come from the same Jelly Roll. You can mix and match the greens or reds or aquas from multiple Jelly Rolls to make your own custom scrap mix. It's easy. And fun. And a new way of thinking. Here are some more guidelines I like to follow when working with these precut strips with pinked edges.

"I sometimes call for a certain number of strips of each color."

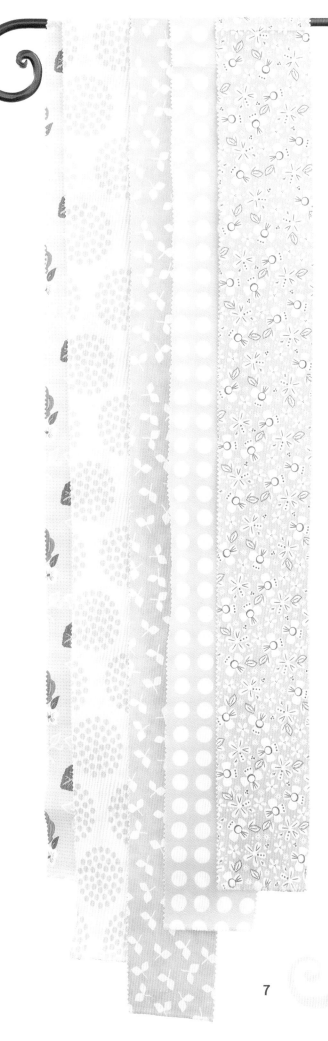

7

ELIMINATE THE FUZZ. Before strip piecing with Jelly Roll strips, I take them one at a time, folded from selvage to selvage, and measure to make sure each strip is 2½" wide. Then ever-so-carefully I lay my ruler on top and trim off the fuzzy edges with my rotary cutter. Brush the bits of fabric lint into the wastebasket and then you only have to deal with that once—not every time you pick up your blocks.

"Then ever-so-carefully I lay my ruler on top and trim off the fuzzy edges with my rotary cutter."

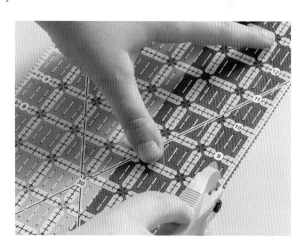

USE A COLLAPSIBLE DRYING RACK. When working on a project with tons of strips, draping them over a collapsible drying rack is an excellent way to corral them. They'll all be readily visible and at the ready, rather than piled up and wrinkled.

HOLD 'EM STEADY. When joining long strips, hold the strips together firmly in front of and behind the needle. Do not pull or stretch them; simply holding them firmly will prevent puckered stitches or bowed strip sets.

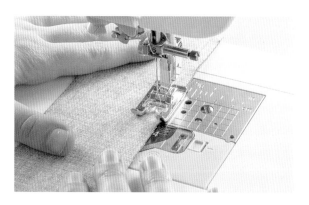

The Easy Angle Ruler

While it's easy to make gorgeous Jelly Roll quilts that contain only squares and rectangles (see Sea Glass on page 64 for a great example of this), using half-square triangles really expands the design possibilities (see Cherry Orchard on page 26). In order to cut half-square triangles from the same strip width (2½") I use to cut squares and rectangles, I cut off the dog-ears from the triangles with an Easy Angle ruler. To use this acrylic tool, be sure the left edge of your strip is straight, then line up the 2½" lines of the ruler along the left and top edges of the strip. Rotary cut along the angled edge to cut one triangle with a blunted tip at the top.

"...using half-square triangles really expands the design possibilities."

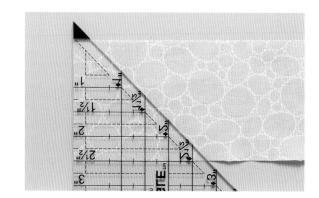

Then rotate the tool 180° to cut another triangle, this one with a blunted tip at the bottom.

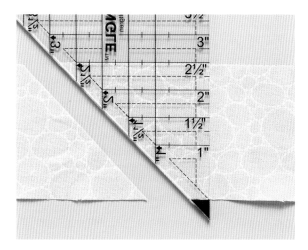

If you don't want to buy an Easy Angle ruler, I've provided a pattern with each project that uses half-square triangles. Just make a template from the pattern and trace it onto your strip as described above, then cut out with scissors or a rotary cutter.

Have Fun!

Somebody once asked me what my best weekend smelled like. The first thing that came to mind was suntan lotion and salty beach air. I have realized that most of the time, the colors I quilt with remind me of being at the beach or on an island. I love a quilt that mushes colors all together while creating a soft, gently used look at the same time. Whatever your preferred color scheme, I hope you'll consider mixing and matching precuts. I think you'll be pleasantly surprised by the results, and in the end, you'll have a custom-blended scrap quilt to show for it!

"...I hope you'll consider mixing and matching precuts."

Airboats

I may have taken the long way around when creating this block, but at first I couldn't find a size or construction method that seemed simple enough that I'd want to continue making lots of these! That's why the block is constructed the way it is. The design itself reminds me of an airboat ride my family and I took in the Florida Everglades.

QUILT SIZE: 77⅛" × 94⅛"
BLOCK SIZE: 10" × 10"

Materials

Yardage is based on 42"-wide fabric unless otherwise noted.

48 strips, 2½" × 42", of assorted medium to dark prints in turquoise, red, green, orange, blue, pink, and yellow for blocks

3¾ yards of cream solid for blocks

16 squares, 10" × 10", of assorted light to medium prints in red, turquoise, blue, orange, and green for blocks

3½ yards of aqua floral for sashing squares, setting triangles, border, and binding

2⅛ yards of orange check for sashing rectangles

¼ yard of orange solid for sashing squares

7¼ yards of fabric for backing

86" × 103" piece of batting

Easy Dresden tool *OR* template plastic

Cutting

All measurements include ¼" seam allowances. To cut wedges for the blocks from 2½"-wide strips, I use the 5" line on the Easy Dresden acrylic tool. If you prefer, trace the wedge pattern on page 14 onto template plastic and cut out the shape on the drawn lines. Trace the template onto the wrong side of the 2½" × 5" rectangles specified below to make the required number of wedges.

From *each* of 32 medium or dark print strips, cut:

8 rectangles, 2½" × 5"; cut each rectangle into a wedge using Easy Dresden or wedge pattern (256 total)

From *each* of the 16 remaining medium or dark print strips, cut:

8 rectangles, 2" × 4¾" (128 total)

From the cream solid, cut:

48 strips, 2½" × 42; crosscut into 384 rectangles, 2½" × 5". Cut each rectangle into a wedge using Easy Dresden or wedge pattern.

From *each* of the 16 light or medium print squares, cut:

4 squares, 3½" × 3½"; cut the squares in half diagonally to yield 8 triangles (128 total)

2 squares, 2" × 2" (32 total)

Continued on page 12

Susan says...

This quilt isn't about matching colors, but rather it's about the contrast in values. Each block takes three fabrics, so figure out how many total fabrics you have to work with and then divide them into groups of three. Each group doesn't have to be your favorite color combination—the colors just have to contrast with one another to make the blocks work.

Continued from page 10

From the aqua floral, cut:

2 strips, 18½" × 42"; crosscut into 4 squares, 18½" × 18½". Cut the squares into quarters diagonally to yield 16 side triangles (2 will be extra).

1 strip, 11" × 42"; crosscut into 2 squares, 11" × 11". Cut the squares in half diagonally to yield 4 corner triangles.

9 strips, 3½" × 42"

13 strips, 2½" × 42"; crosscut *3 of the strips* into 31 squares, 2½" × 2½"

From the orange check, cut:

27 strips, 2½" × 42"; crosscut into 80 strips, 2½" × 10½"

From the orange solid, cut:

2 strips, 2½" × 42"; crosscut into 18 squares, 2½" × 2½"

Making the Blocks

Press the seam allowances as indicated by the arrows.

1 Sew together three cream wedges and two matching print wedges as shown to make a wedge unit. Repeat to make 128 wedge units (32 sets of 4 matching units).

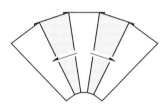

Wedge unit.
Make 32 matching sets of 4 (128 total).

2 Position a light or medium print triangle on a wedge unit, right sides together, with the long edge of the triangle ⅜" above the bottom edge of the center wedge. Sew together ¼" from the long edge of the triangle. Flip the triangle right side up and press. Repeat to add a matching triangle to three more matching wedge units.

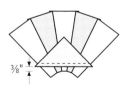 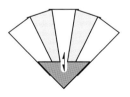

Make 4.

3 Lay out the four wedge units, a matching print 2" square, and four medium or dark 2" × 4¾" rectangles from another print in three rows as shown. Aligning the seams, sew together the pieces in each row. Join the rows to complete the block.

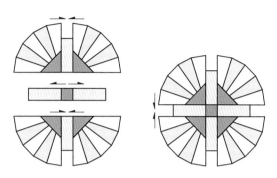

4 Trim the block so it measures 10½" square, including seam allowances. Make 32 blocks.

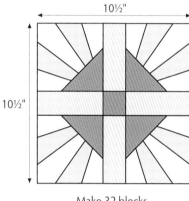

Make 32 blocks.
Trim to 10½" × 10½".

Susan says...

Don't be intimidated by the fans in this block. Once you piece them together, you assemble the block just like a Nine Patch and then simply square up the block. Take your time and the whole thing will magically come together!

Assembling the Quilt Top

1 Referring to the quilt assembly diagram, lay out the blocks, orange check sashing rectangles, orange solid and aqua floral sashing squares, and aqua floral setting triangles in diagonal rows. Note that the setting triangles are oversized and will be trimmed after assembly. Sew together the blocks and sashing pieces in each row.

2 Join each block row and its adjacent sashing row as shown. Add the side setting triangles to each end of the block rows. Join the rows, and add the corner triangles last. Carefully trim the excess from the setting triangles, ¼" beyond the points of the sashing squares. The quilt top should measure 71⅛" × 88⅛", including seam allowances.

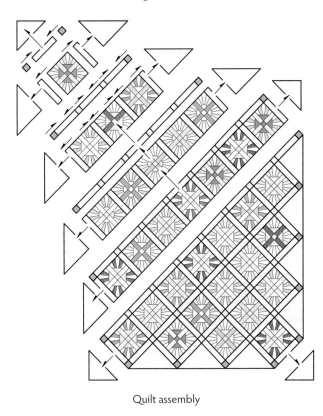

Quilt assembly

3 Join the aqua floral 3½" × 42" strips end to end and press the seam allowances open. Trim the pieced length into two 88⅛"-long border strips and two 77⅛"-long border strips. Sew the longer strips to the sides of the quilt top and press the seam allowances toward the borders. Sew the shorter strips to the top and bottom edges of the quilt top and press the seam allowances toward the borders. The completed quilt top should measure 77⅛" × 94⅛".

Finishing the Quilt

If you need detailed instructions about any of the finishing steps, go to ShopMartingale.com for free downloadable information.

1 Prepare the quilt backing so it is about 8" larger in both directions than the quilt top.

2 Layer the backing, batting, and quilt top. Baste the layers together.

3 Hand or machine quilt as desired; the quilt shown was quilted with an allover spiral design.

4 Using the aqua floral 2½"-wide strips, make the binding and attach it to the quilt.

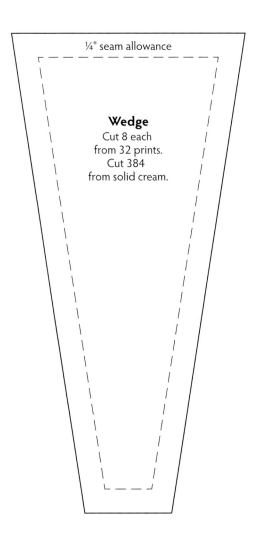

¼" seam allowance

Wedge
Cut 8 each
from 32 prints.
Cut 384
from solid cream.

Beach Reading

As a born-and-raised Floridian, I always have on hand a beach-go bag filled with a quilt, a book, sunscreen, a towel, and a jug of water to rinse my feet. This quilt will ride in the back of the car throughout the entire beach season! I loved the idea of text-motif fabric mixed with solids, and this is perfect for that beachy look.

QUILT SIZE: 76½" × 76½"
BLOCK SIZE: 8" × 8"

Materials

Yardage is based on 42"-wide fabric unless otherwise noted. Fat eighths are 9" × 21".

34 strips, 2½" × 42", of assorted solids for blocks and border

34 strips, 2½" × 42", of assorted black-and-white prints for blocks and border

1¼ yards of black-and-white polka dot for setting triangles

⅞ yard of black-and-white stripe for border and binding

6 fat eighths of assorted stripes for border*

7¼ yards of fabric for backing

85" × 85" square of batting

*What appear to be pieced rectangles in the center of the border strips are actually segments of a multicolored stripe. If you're using a similar fabric, you'll need only ⅝ yard total.

Cutting

All measurements include ¼" seam allowances.

From the black-and-white polka dot, cut:

1 square, 25" × 25"; cut the square into quarters diagonally to yield 4 large side triangles

2 squares, 13" × 13"; cut the squares into quarters diagonally to yield 8 small side triangles

2 squares, 13" × 13"; cut the squares in half diagonally to yield 4 corner triangles

From the black-and-white stripe, cut:

2 rectangles, 4½" × 8½"

2 squares, 4½" × 4½"

Enough 2½"-wide bias strips to total 325" in length for binding

From the assorted stripes, cut a *total* of:

6 rectangles, 4½" × 8½"

6 squares, 4½" × 4½"

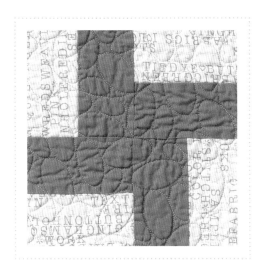

Making the Blocks and Border Segments

Press the seam allowances as indicated by the arrows.

1 Sew together a solid-color 2½" × 42" strip and a black-and-white print 2½" × 42" strip to make a strip set. Press the seam allowances toward the solid color. Repeat to make 34 strip sets that measure 4½" × 42".

2 From *22* of the strip sets, crosscut eight 4½"-wide block segments and one 2½"-wide border segment, for a total of 176 block segments and 22 border segments (10 will be extra).

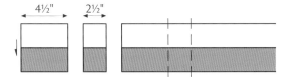

From each of *22* strip sets,
cut 8 segments, 4½", and 1 segment 2½".

3 From the remaining *12* strip sets, crosscut four 4½"-wide block segments and seven 2½"-wide border segments, for a total of 48 block segments and 84 border segments. Combined with the units from step 2, you should now have 224 block segments and 106 border segments.

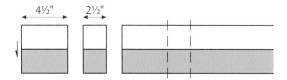

From each of *12* strip sets,
cut 4 segments, 4½", and 7 segments 2½".

4 Lay out four matching block segments in two rows as shown. Sew together the block segments in each row, and then join the rows to complete the block. The block should measure 8½" square, including seam allowances. Repeat to make 56 blocks.

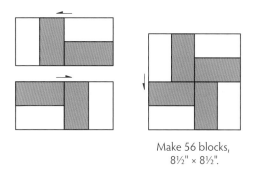

Make 56 blocks,
8½" × 8½".

Assembling the Quilt Top

1 Referring to the quilt assembly diagram on page 18, lay out the blocks, large and small polka-dot side triangles, and polka-dot corner triangles in diagonal rows. Note that the setting triangles are oversized and will be trimmed after assembly. Sew together the blocks in each row.

2 Join the adjacent pairs of rows as shown. Sew the small side triangles to each end of the single block rows, and sew the large side triangles and two of the corner triangles to the pairs of block rows. Join the rows and add the remaining corner triangles.

Quilt assembly

3 Carefully trim the excess from the setting triangles, ¼" beyond the points of the blocks. The quilt top should measure 68½" square, including seam allowances.

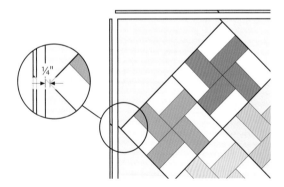

Trim ¼" past points of blocks.

Adding the Border

1 Lay out 22 border segments, one black-and-white stripe 4½" square, one stripe 4½" square, and two assorted stripe 4½" × 8½" rectangles in a row as shown. Sew the pieces together to make the top border. The border should measure 4½" × 68½", including seam allowances. Repeat to make the bottom border.

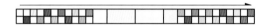

Top/bottom border.
Make 2, 4½" × 68½".

2 Lay out 26 pieced border segments, two assorted stripe 4½" squares, one black-and-white stripe 4½" × 8½" rectangle, and one stripe 4½" × 8½" rectangle in a row as shown. Sew the pieces together to make a side border. The border should measure 4½" × 76½", including seam allowances. Repeat to make a second side border.

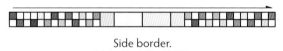

Side border.
Make 2, 4½" × 76½".

3 Sew the top and bottom borders to the quilt top, and then add the side borders. The completed quilt top should measure 76½" square.

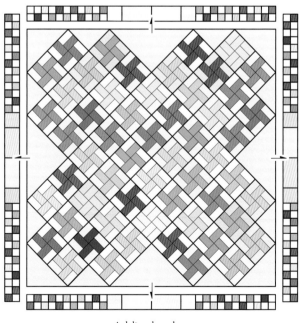

Adding borders

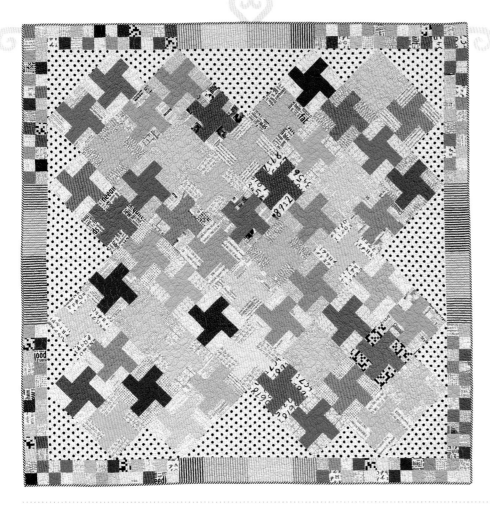

Susan says...

When it comes to text prints, don't be afraid to cut them up and turn them every which way in a quilt design. Here they're used as the background, where they look fabulous and act as a foil for the solids, the stars of the show.

Finishing the Quilt

If you need detailed instructions about any of the finishing steps, go to ShopMartingale.com for free downloadable information.

1 Prepare the quilt backing so it is about 8" larger in both directions than the quilt top.

2 Layer the backing, batting, and quilt top. Baste the layers together.

3 Hand or machine quilt as desired; the quilt shown was quilted with an allover oval design.

4 Using the black-and-white stripe 2½"-wide bias strips, make the binding and attach it to the quilt.

Stargazing

I had been wanting a zigzag quilt, and Stargazing happened rather spontaneously while I was making Star blocks. I realized a soft tan would show off the blocks beautifully.

QUILT SIZE: 81½" × 81½"
BLOCK SIZE: 9¾" × 9¾"

Materials

Yardage is based on 42"-wide fabric unless otherwise noted. Fat quarters are 18"×21".

27 strips, 2½" × 42", of assorted medium and dark prints for blocks*

13 fat quarters of assorted light prints for block backgrounds

5⅛ yards of tan floral for setting triangles, inner and outer borders, and binding

⅜ yard of cream solid for middle border

7½ yards of fabric for backing

90" × 90" piece of batting

Acrylic ruler with 45° marking

I didn't want to repeat prints in more than one block, so I used 54 different strips.

Cutting

All measurements include ¼" seam allowances.

From the assorted medium and dark prints, cut a *total* of:

54 strips, 2½" × 20"

From *each* of the 13 light prints, cut:

8 squares, 3¾" × 3¾"; cut the squares in half diagonally to yield 16 large triangles (208 total; 8 will be extra)

8 squares, 2⅞" × 2⅞"; cut the squares in half diagonally to yield 16 small triangles (208 total; 8 will be extra)

From the tan floral, cut:

6 strips, 15½" × 42"; cut into:

♦ 11 squares, 15½" × 15½"; cut the squares into quarters diagonally to yield 44 side triangles

♦ 6 squares, 8¼" × 8¼"; cut the squares in half diagonally to yield 12 corner triangles

9 strips, 3½" × 42"

17 strips, 2½" × 42"

From the cream solid, cut:

8 strips, 1½" × 42"

Making the Blocks

Press the seam allowances as indicated by the arrows.

1. Using a rotary cutter, mat, and the 45° line on an acrylic ruler, trim one end of a medium or dark 2½" × 20" strip at a 45° angle.

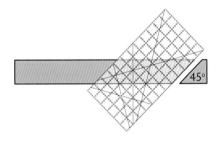

2. Rotate the strip so the cut edge is on your left. Cutting parallel to the trimmed edge, cut four diamonds, 2½" wide.

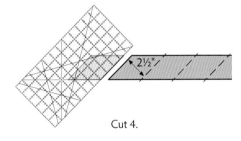

Cut 4.

3. Repeat steps 1 and 2 to cut 54 sets of four matching diamonds.

4. For one Star block, gather two sets of four matching diamonds, as well as eight large triangles and eight small triangles from one light print.

5. Sew a small triangle to the top-left edge of a diamond as shown. Add a large triangle to the top-right edge to make a star-point unit. Repeat to make four matching star-point units.

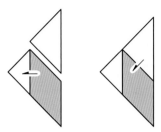

Make 4 star-point units.

6. Adding the triangles to the reverse edges of the diamond, repeat step 5 to make four mirror-image star-point units.

Make 4 mirror-image star-point units.

7. Sew together a star-point unit and a mirror-image star-point unit to make a quarter block. The block should measure 5⅜" square, including seam allowances. Repeat to make four matching quarter blocks.

Make 4 quarter blocks, 5⅜" × 5⅜".

Susan says...

I usually work in soft colors, but I was determined to jump in the deep end and use the black and navy prints from a Jelly Roll. The secret to making it work? Use the same number of strips of each color so the shades can be distributed around the quilt. If you're using three red strips, then use three blacks, three aquas, and so on.

8 Lay out the quarter blocks in two rows of two. Sew the blocks into rows, and then join the rows to complete a Star block. The block should measure 10¼" square, including seam allowances. Make 23 Star blocks.

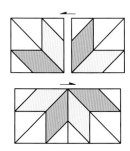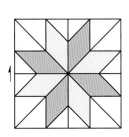

Make 23 star blocks,
10¼" × 10¼".

9 For a half Star block, gather two pairs of matching diamonds, as well as four large triangles and four small triangles from one light print.

10 Using the gathered pieces, repeat step 5 to make two star-point units, and repeat step 6 to make two mirror-image star-point units.

11 Repeat step 7 to make a quarter block. Sew the star-point unit and mirror-image star-point unit to adjacent edges of the quarter block to make a half Star block. Make four half Star blocks.

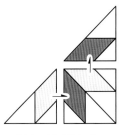

Make 4 half blocks.

Assembling the Quilt Top

1 Lay out five on-point Star blocks, eight tan side setting triangles, and four tan corner setting triangles as shown. Note that the setting triangles are slightly oversized and will be trimmed after assembly. Sew together the blocks and side triangles in diagonal rows, and then join the rows. Add the corner triangles last to complete an odd-numbered row. Repeat to make three odd-numbered rows.

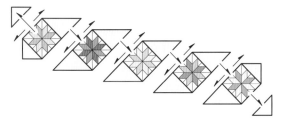

Odd-numbered row. Make 3.

2 Lay out four on-point Star blocks, two half Star blocks, and 10 tan side setting triangles as shown. Sew together the blocks and side triangles in diagonal rows, and then join the rows to complete an even-numbered row. Repeat to make two even-numbered rows.

Even-numbered row. Make 2.

3 Carefully trim the excess from the setting triangles, ¼" from the points of the blocks in each row.

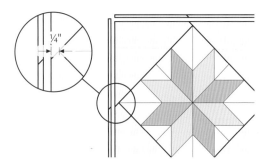

Trim ¼" past points of blocks.

4 Referring to the quilt assembly diagram, sew together the odd- and even-numbered rows in alternating positions. The quilt top should measure 69½" square, including seam allowances.

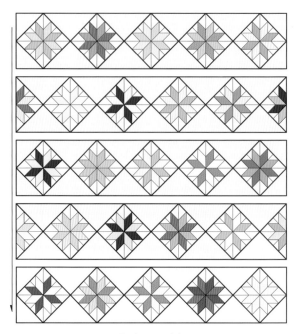

Quilt assembly

Adding the Borders

1 Join eight tan 2½" × 42" strips end to end and press the seam allowances open. Trim the pieced length into two 73½"-long inner-border strips and two 69½"-long inner-border strips. Sew the shorter strips to the sides of the quilt top, and then add the longer strips to the top and bottom edges. The quilt top should now measure 73½" square, including seam allowances.

2 Join the cream 1½" × 42" strips end to end and press the seam allowances open. Trim the pieced length into two 75½"-long middle-border strips and two 73½"-long middle-border strips. Sew the shorter strips to the sides of the quilt top, and then add the longer strips to the top and bottom edges. The quilt top should now measure 75½" square, including seam allowances.

3 Join the tan 3½" × 42" strips end to end and press the seam allowances open. Trim the pieced length into two 81½"-long outer-border strips and two 75½"-long outer-border strips. Sew the shorter strips to the sides of the quilt top, and then add the longer strips to the top and bottom edges. The completed quilt top should measure 81½" square.

Adding borders

Finishing the Quilt

If you need detailed instructions about any of the finishing steps, go to ShopMartingale.com for free downloadable information.

1 Prepare the quilt backing so it is about 8" larger in both directions than the quilt top.

2 Layer the backing, batting, and quilt top. Baste the layers together.

3 Hand or machine quilt as desired; the quilt shown was quilted with parallel lines of stitching that follow the zigzag created by the offset setting triangles. Each block is stitched with a feather design in the star and pebbles in the background.

4 Using the remaining tan floral 2½"-wide strips, make the binding and attach it to the quilt.

Cherry Orchard

I love red-and-green quilts and don't think they should be
reserved just for the holidays. Aside from the borders, there isn't
a single piece in this quilt that doesn't start with a 2½" strip.

QUILT SIZE: 76½" × 76½"
BLOCK SIZE: 14" × 14"

Materials

Yardage is based on 42"-wide fabric unless otherwise noted.

2 strips, 2½" × 42", *each* of 16 assorted red prints for blocks

2 strips, 2½" × 42", *each* of 16 assorted white prints for block backgrounds

16 strips, 2½" × 42", of assorted green prints for blocks

20 strips, 2½" × 42", of light green solid for sashing strips

2 strips, 2½" × 42", of red gingham for sashing squares

2⅛ yards of red floral for border and binding

7¼ yards of fabric for backing

85" × 85" piece of batting

Easy Angle tool *OR* template plastic

Cutting

All measurements include ¼" seam allowances. To cut triangles for the half-square-triangle units from 2½"-wide strips, I use the Easy Angle acrylic tool, which lets you easily cut pieces to make half-square-triangle

units from the same size strip as you cut accompanying squares or rectangles. Or, if you prefer, trace the triangle pattern on page 30 onto template plastic and cut out the shape on the drawn lines. Trace the template onto the wrong side of the 2½"-wide strips specified below, rotating the template 180° after each cut to make the best use of your fabric.

From *each* of the 16 red prints, cut:

1 strip, 2½" × 21" (16 total)

1 square, 2½" × 2½" (16 total)

16 triangles using Easy Angle or triangle pattern (256 total)

From *each* of the 16 white prints, cut:

1 strip, 2½" × 21" (16 total)

4 squares, 2½" × 2½" (64 total)

16 triangles using Easy Angle or triangle pattern (256 total)

From *each* of the 16 green prints, cut:

4 rectangles, 2½" × 6½" (64 total)

From the light green solid, cut:

40 strips, 2½" × 14½"

From the red gingham, cut:

25 squares, 2½" × 2½"

From the red floral, cut:

8 strips, 5½" × 42"

9 strips, 2½" × 42"

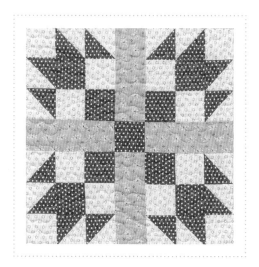

Making the Blocks

Press the seam allowances as indicated by the arrows.

1 Sew together a white triangle and a red triangle to make a half-square-triangle unit. The unit should measure 2½" square, including seam allowances. Repeat to make 16 matching half-square-triangle units.

Make 16,
2½" × 2½".

2 Matching the prints used in step 1, sew together a red 2½" × 21" strip and a white 2½" × 21" strip to make a strip set. Crosscut the strip set into eight segments, 2½" wide.

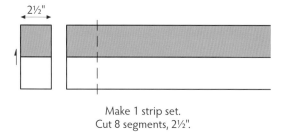

Make 1 strip set.
Cut 8 segments, 2½".

3 Sew together two 2½"-wide segments to make a four-patch unit as shown. Repeat to make four matching units that measure 4½" square, including seam allowances.

Make 4,
4½" × 4½".

4 Lay out four half-square-triangle units, a four-patch unit, and a matching white 2½" square as shown. Join two of the half-square-triangle units in a vertical row, and sew the row to the left edge of the four-patch unit. Join the remaining half-square-triangle units and the white square in a horizontal row, and sew the row to the top edge of the four-patch unit to complete a quarter block. The quarter block should measure 6½" square, including seam allowances. Repeat to make four matching quarter blocks.

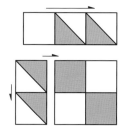 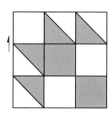

Make 4,
6½" × 6½".

Susan says...

Looking for a great seasonal project? This quilt is it! Choose two colors and a background and you could make this for any holiday or time of year. Black, orange, and gray for Halloween; rust, avocado, and gold for fall—or simply choose your favorite color scheme and enjoy this beauty all year long.

5 Lay out four quarter blocks, one matching red 2½" square, and four matching green 2½" × 6½" rectangles in three rows. Sew together the pieces in each row. Join the rows to complete a block that measures 14½" square, including seam allowances. Make 16 blocks.

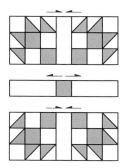

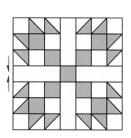

Make 16 blocks,
14½" × 14½".

Assembling the Quilt Top

1 Lay out the blocks in four rows of four blocks each, adding the light green sashing rectangles and red gingham sashing squares as shown in the quilt assembly diagram. Sew together the blocks and sashing pieces in each row, and then join the rows. The quilt top should measure 66½" square, including seam allowances.

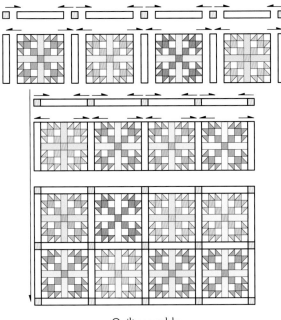

Quilt assembly

2 Join the red floral 5½" × 42" strips end to end and press the seam allowances open. Trim the pieced length into two 76½"-long border strips and two 66½"-long border strips. Sew the shorter strips to the sides of the quilt top and press the seam allowances toward the borders. Sew the longer strips to the top and bottom edges of the quilt top and press the seam allowances toward the borders. The completed quilt top should measure 76½" square.

Finishing the Quilt

If you need detailed instructions about any of the finishing steps, go to ShopMartingale.com for free downloadable information.

1 Prepare the quilt backing so it is about 8" larger in both directions than the quilt top.

2 Layer the backing, batting, and quilt top. Baste the layers together.

3 Hand or machine quilt as desired; the quilt shown was quilted with an allover floral design.

4 Using the red floral 2½"-wide strips, make the binding and attach it to the quilt.

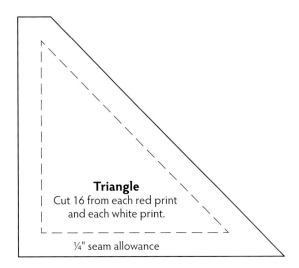

Triangle
Cut 16 from each red print
and each white print.

¼" seam allowance

Four Square

This Four Square design reminds me of the way tables are laid out in a cafeteria. The nine-patches are made with leftovers from the Roman Cross blocks. The Roman Cross block is actually the same as a Churn Dash block, just with different color placement.

QUILT SIZE: 67⅞" × 84⅞"
BLOCK SIZE: 6" × 6"

Materials

Yardage is based on 42"-wide fabric unless otherwise noted.

2 strips, 2½" × 42", *each of 32* assorted medium to dark prints in green, red, blue, and pink (collectively referred to as "dark prints") for blocks

6⅝ yards of mottled light aqua for blocks, setting triangles, border, and binding

5¼ yards of fabric for backing

76" × 93" piece of batting

Easy Angle tool *OR* template plastic

Cutting

All measurements include ¼" seam allowances. To cut triangles for the half-square-triangle units from 2½"-wide strips, I use the Easy Angle acrylic tool. If you prefer, trace the triangle pattern on page 35 onto template plastic and cut out the shape on the drawn lines. Trace the template onto the wrong side of the 2½"-wide strips specified below, rotating the template 180° after each cut to make the best use of your fabric.

From *each of 16* assorted dark prints, cut:

2 squares, 2½" × 2½" (32 total)

8 triangles using Easy Angle or triangle pattern (128 total)

1 strip, 1½" × 21" (16 total)

1 strip, 1½" × 18"; crosscut into:

- ◆ 2 strips, 1½" × 5" (32 total)
- ◆ 4 squares, 1½" × 1½" (64 total)

From *each of the 16* remaining dark prints, cut:

2 squares, 2½" × 2½" (32 total)

8 triangles using Easy Angle or triangle pattern (128 total)

1 strip, 1½" × 21" (16 total)

1 strip, 1½" × 9"; crosscut into:

- ◆ 1 strip, 1½" × 5" (16 total)
- ◆ 2 squares, 1½" × 1½" (32 total)

Continued on page 33

Continued from page 31

From the mottled light aqua, cut:

3 strips, 10¼" × 42"; crosscut into:

- 7 squares, 10¼" × 10¼". Cut the squares into quarters diagonally to yield 28 side triangles.
- 2 squares, 5½" × 5½". Cut the squares in half diagonally to yield 4 corner triangles.

8 strips, 4½" × 42"

20 strips, 2½" × 42"; crosscut *11 of the strips* into a total of 256 triangles using Easy Angle or triangle pattern

25 strips, 2" × 42"; crosscut into:

- 96 rectangles, 2" × 6½"
- 96 rectangles, 2" × 3½"

32 strips, 1½" × 42"; crosscut into:

- 32 strips, 1½" × 21"
- 48 strips, 1½" × 5"
- 48 squares, 1½" × 1½"

Making the Roman Cross Blocks

Press the seam allowances as indicated by the arrows.

1 Sew together a dark triangle and a light aqua triangle to make a half-square-triangle unit. The unit should measure 2½" square, including seam allowances. Repeat to make eight matching half-square-triangle units.

Make 8,
2½" × 2½".

2 Matching the print used in step 1, sew together a dark 1½" × 21" strip and a light aqua 1½" × 21" strip to make a strip set. Crosscut the strip set into eight segments, 2½" wide.

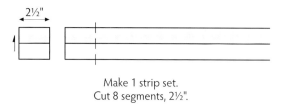

2½"

Make 1 strip set.
Cut 8 segments, 2½".

3 Lay out four half-square-triangle units, four 2½"-wide segments, and one matching dark 2½" square in three rows as shown. Sew together the pieces in each row, and then join the rows to complete a Roman Cross block. The block should measure 6½" square, including seam allowances. Repeat to make a second matching Roman Cross block.

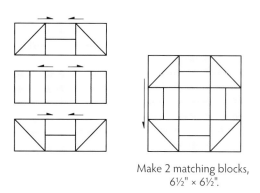

Make 2 matching blocks,
6½" × 6½".

4 Repeat steps 1–3 to make 64 Roman Cross blocks (you will use 63 and have 1 left over to add to your stash if you wish).

Making the Bordered Nine Patch Blocks

1 Sew together a dark 1½" × 5" strip and a light aqua 1½" × 5" strip to make a strip set. Crosscut the strip set into three segments, 1½" wide.

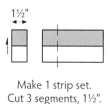

1½"

Make 1 strip set.
Cut 3 segments, 1½".

Susan says...

This may become your go-to pattern, it's that versatile and that easy. Omit the green for a nautical theme, or switch to red and green for a Christmas quilt. Or make it smaller for a baby quilt.

2 Lay out three 1½"-wide segments, two matching dark 1½" squares, and one light aqua 1½" square in three rows as shown. Sew together the pieces in each row, and then join the rows to make a nine-patch unit. The unit should measure 3½" square, including seam allowances.

3 Repeat steps 1 and 2 to make 48 nine-patch units.

4 Sew light aqua 2" × 3½" rectangles to the sides of a nine-patch unit. Add light aqua 2" × 6½" rectangles to the top and bottom edges to make a

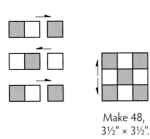

Make 48,
3½" × 3½".

Bordered Nine Patch block. The block should measure 6½" square, including seam allowances. Repeat to make 48 Bordered Nine Patch blocks.

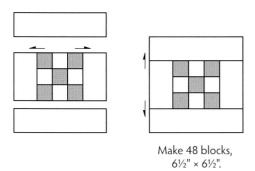

Make 48 blocks,
6½" × 6½".

Assembling the Quilt Top

1 Referring to the quilt assembly diagram, lay out the blocks and light aqua setting triangles in diagonal rows. Note that the setting triangles are oversized and will be trimmed after assembly. Sew together the blocks and side triangles in each row, and then join the rows. Press the seam allowances in one direction. Add the corner triangles last. Carefully trim the excess from the setting triangles, ¼" beyond the points of the blocks. The quilt top should measure 59⅞" × 76⅞", including seam allowances.

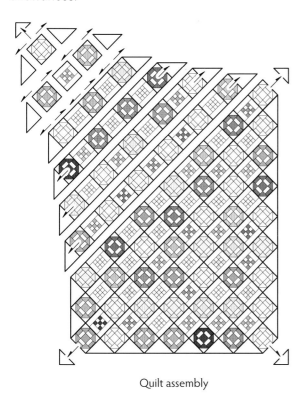

Quilt assembly

2 Join the light aqua 4½" × 42" strips end to end and press the seam allowances open. Trim the pieced length into two 76⅞"-long border strips and two 67⅞"-long border strips. Sew the longer strips to the sides of the quilt top and press the seam allowances toward the borders. Sew the shorter strips to the top and bottom edges of the quilt top and press the seam allowances toward the borders. The completed quilt top should measure 67⅞" × 84⅞".

Finishing the Quilt

If you need detailed instructions about any of the finishing steps, go to ShopMartingale.com for free downloadable information.

1 Prepare the quilt backing so it is about 8" larger in both directions than the quilt top.

2 Layer the backing, batting, and quilt top. Baste the layers together.

3 Hand or machine quilt as desired; the quilt shown was quilted with allover stippling stitched in a square spiral design.

4 Using the remaining light aqua 2½"-wide strips, make the binding and attach it to the quilt.

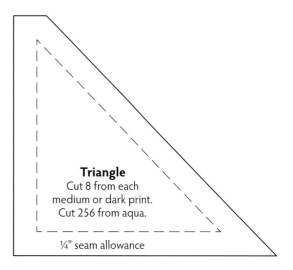

Triangle
Cut 8 from each medium or dark print.
Cut 256 from aqua.

¼" seam allowance

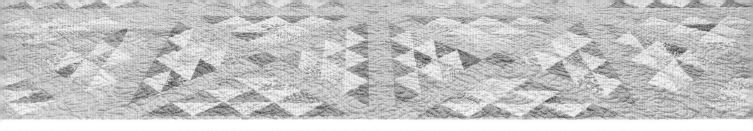

Citrus Grove

I make no secret of the fact that I love orange, especially in vintage Florida postcards. The pairing of orange and pink is, to me, one of the prettiest combos there is. Growing up in Florida, I played many games of tag in the orange and grapefruit groves, where the colors were glorious and we could pick and eat the fruit right from the tree.

QUILT SIZE: 72" × 72"
BLOCK SIZE: 13½" × 13½"

Materials

Yardage is based on 42"-wide fabric unless otherwise noted.

16 strips, 2½" × 42", of assorted orange and pink prints for blocks

16 strips, 2½" × 42", of assorted light prints for blocks

16 strips, 2½" × 42", of assorted orange and pink solids and tone on tones for blocks

2⅛ yards of green print for blocks and sashing

1¼ yards of orange floral for border

⅔ yard of coral solid for binding

5 yards of fabric for backing

80" × 80" piece of batting

Easy Angle tool *OR* template plastic

Cutting

All measurements include ¼" seam allowances. To cut triangles for the half-square-triangle units from 2½"-wide strips, I use the Easy Angle acrylic tool. If you prefer, trace the triangle pattern on page 40 onto template plastic and cut out the shape on the drawn lines. Trace the template onto the wrong side of the 2½"-wide strips specified below, rotating the template 180° after each cut to make the best use of your fabric.

From *each* of the 16 orange and pink print strips, cut:

24 triangles using Easy Angle or triangle pattern (384 total)

From *each* of the 16 light print strips, cut:

24 triangles using Easy Angle or triangle pattern (384 total)

From *each* of the 16 orange and pink solid or tone-on-tone strips, cut:

16 triangles using Easy Angle or triangle pattern (256 total)

1 square, 2" × 2" (16 total)

Continued on page 38

Continued from page 36

From the green print, cut:

34 strips, 2" × 42"; crosscut *22 of the strips* into:

- ◆ 12 rectangles, 2" × 14"*
- ◆ 64 strips, 2" × 10"

From the orange floral, cut:

7 strips, 5½" × 42"

From the coral solid, cut:

8 strips, 2½" × 42"

*These rectangles will be used for sashing, but because it's easy to end up with blocks that are a bit larger or smaller than they should be, I suggest you wait to cut these rectangles until you have completed and measured your blocks.

Making the Blocks

Press the seam allowances as indicated by the arrows.

1 Sew together an orange or pink print triangle and a light print triangle to make a half-square-triangle unit. The unit should measure 2½" square, including seam allowances. Repeat to make 384 half-square-triangle units.

Make 384,
2½" × 2½".

2 Lay out four matching tone-on-tone or solid triangles and six assorted half-square-triangle units in four rows as shown. Sew together the pieces in each row, and then join the rows to complete a triangle unit. Repeat to make 64 triangle units.

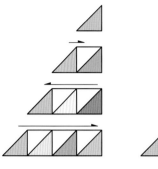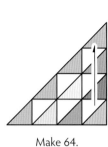

Make 64.

3 Referring to the block assembly diagram, lay out four triangle units (all with the same tone on tone or solid), a matching tone-on-tone or solid 2" square, and four green 2" × 10" strips in three rows. Sew together the pieces in each row, and then join the rows to complete the block. As you press, be very careful not to stretch the block edges, which are on the bias.

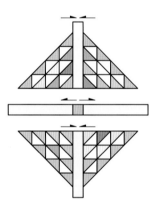

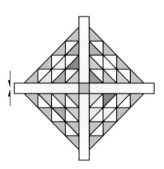

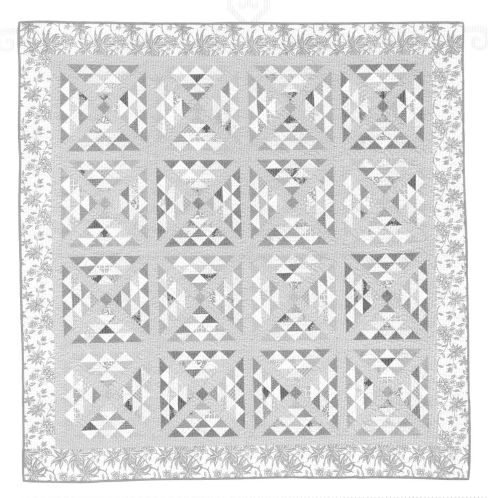

Susan says...

After my blocks were
constructed, I trimmed
them all to 14" square.
Because the block edges
are on the bias, your
blocks may end up a
little larger or smaller
than mine. The most
important things are to
trim blocks to a uniform
size and to be sure to
leave a ¼" seam
allowance all the way
around when you trim.

4 Trim away the excess from the green strips at
the block corners and square up the block to 14"
square, including seam allowances. Make 16 blocks.

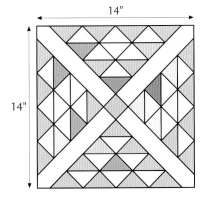

Make 16 blocks.
Trim each to 14" × 14".

Assembling the Quilt Top

1 Join the remaining green 2" × 42" strips end to
end and press the seam allowances open. Trim
the pieced length into five 59"-long sashing strips
and two 62"-long sashing strips.

2 Lay out the blocks in four rows of four blocks
each, adding the green 2" × 14" sashing
rectangles and the 59"-long sashing strips as shown
in the quilt assembly diagram. Sew the pieces
together in each block row, and then join the block
rows and vertical sashing strips. Add the 62"-long

sashing strips to the top and bottom edges. The quilt top should now measure 62" square, including seam allowances.

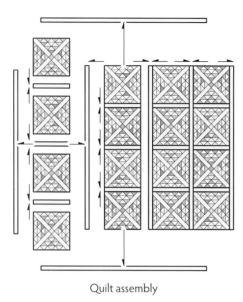

Quilt assembly

3 Join the orange floral 5½" × 42" strips end to end and press the seam allowances open. Trim the pieced length into two 72"-long border strips and two 62"-long border strips. Sew the shorter strips to the sides of the quilt top and press the seam allowances toward the borders. Sew the longer strips to the top and bottom edges and press the seam allowances toward the borders. The completed quilt top should measure 72" square.

Finishing the Quilt

If you need detailed instructions about any of the finishing steps, go to ShopMartingale.com for free downloadable information.

1 Prepare the quilt backing so it is about 8" larger in both directions than the quilt top.

2 Layer the backing, batting, and quilt top. Baste the layers together.

3 Hand or machine quilt as desired; the quilt shown was quilted with an allover spiral-and-circle design.

4 Using the coral 2½"-wide strips, make the binding and attach it to the quilt.

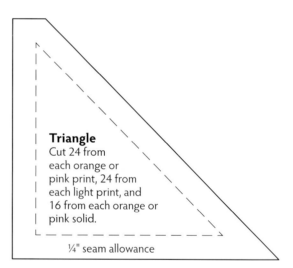

Triangle
Cut 24 from each orange or pink print, 24 from each light print, and 16 from each orange or pink solid.

¼" seam allowance

Churned Around

I adore medallion quilts and I also adore red-and-white
color schemes, so this was a simple, striking way
to combine two of my loves in one project.

QUILT SIZE: 73⅝" × 73⅝"
BLOCK SIZE: 6" × 6"

Materials

*Yardage is based on 42"-wide fabric unless otherwise
noted.*

41 strips, 2½" × 42", *OR* 2⅔ yards total of red solid
for Churn Dash blocks, sashing, and inner and
outer borders

4 yards of white solid for Churn Dash blocks,
sashing squares, X blocks and units, setting
triangles, and middle border

2⅛ yards of red gingham for X blocks and units,
middle border, and binding

7 strips, 2½" × 42", *OR* ⅝ yard total of red-and-
white dot for X blocks and units and middle
border

6⅞ yards of fabric for backing

82" × 82" piece of batting

Easy Angle tool *OR* template plastic

Cutting

*All measurements include ¼" seam allowances. To
cut triangles for the half-square-triangle units from
2½"-wide strips, I use the Easy Angle acrylic tool. If
you prefer, trace the triangle pattern on page 47 onto
template plastic and cut out the shape on the drawn
lines. Trace the template onto the wrong side of the
2½"-wide strips specified below, rotating the template
180° after each cut to make the best use of your fabric.*

From the red solid, cut:

9 strips, 2½" × 42"; crosscut into:

- 100 triangles using Easy Angle or triangle
  pattern
- 100 rectangles, 1½" × 2½"

32 strips, 2" × 42"; crosscut *18 of the strips* into:

- 2 strips, 2" × 39½"
- 4 strips, 2" × 36½"
- 4 strips, 2" × 24½"
- 2 strips, 2" × 21½"
- 4 strips, 2" × 9½"
- 40 strips, 2" × 6½"

Continued on page 43

Continued from page 41

From the white solid, cut:

2 strips, 13" × 42"; cut into:

- ◆ 4 squares, 13" × 13"; cut the squares into quarters diagonally to yield 16 side triangles
- ◆ 2 squares, 9" × 9"; cut the squares in half diagonally to yield 4 corner triangles

2 strips, 6½" × 42"; crosscut into:

- ◆ 4 rectangles, 6½" × 10⅝"
- ◆ 4 rectangles, 4⅝" × 6½"

18 strips, 3½" × 42"

14 strips, 2½" × 42"; crosscut into:

- ◆ 24 rectangles, 2½" × 4½"
- ◆ 25 squares, 2½" × 2½"
- ◆ 100 triangles using Easy Angle or triangle pattern
- ◆ 4 squares, 2" × 2"
- ◆ 100 rectangles, 1½" × 2½"

From the red gingham, cut:

16 strips, 2½" × 42"

Enough 2½"-wide bias strips to total 315" in length for binding

From the red-and-white dot, cut:

7 strips, 2½" × 42"

Making the Churn Dash Blocks

Press the seam allowances as indicated by the arrows.

1 Sew together a red triangle and a white triangle to make a half-square-triangle unit. The unit should measure 2½" square, including seam allowances. Repeat to make 100 half-square-triangle units.

Make 100,
2½" × 2½".

2 Sew together a red 1½" × 2½" rectangle and a white 1½" × 2½" rectangle to make a side unit. The unit should measure 2½" square, including seam allowances. Repeat to make 100 side units.

Make 100 side units,
2½" × 2½".

3 Lay out four half-square-triangle units, four side units, and one white 2½" square in three rows as shown. Join the pieces in each row, and then join the rows to complete a Churn Dash block. The block should measure 6½" square, including seam allowances. Repeat to make 25 Churn Dash blocks.

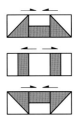

Make 25 blocks,
6½" × 6½".

Assembling the Quilt Center

Referring to the diagram below, lay out 12 red 2" × 6½" sashing strips, nine Churn Dash blocks, and the four white 2" squares in five rows. Sew together the pieces in each row, and then join the rows. The completed quilt center should measure 21½" square, including seam allowances.

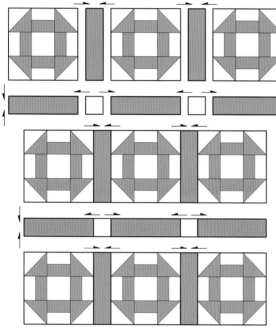
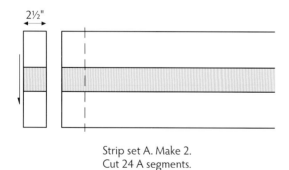

Quilt center assembly

Making the X Blocks and Units

1 Sew together two white 3½" × 42" strips and one red gingham 2½" × 42" strip as shown to make strip set A. Repeat to make a second strip set. Crosscut the strip sets into a total of 24 A segments, 2½" wide.

2½"

Strip set A. Make 2.
Cut 24 A segments.

2 Sew together two white 3½" × 42" strips, two red gingham 2½" × 42" strips, and one red-and-white dot 2½" × 42" strip as shown to make strip set B. Repeat to make seven strip sets. Crosscut the strip sets into a total of 92 B segments, 2½" wide.

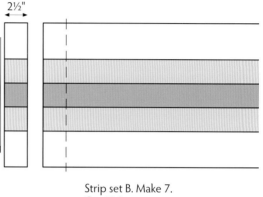

2½"

Strip set B. Make 7.
Cut 92 B segments.

3 Matching the centers of each segment or rectangle, sew together two white 2½" × 4½" rectangles, two A segments, and one B segment as shown. Trim to 6½" square, including seam allowances, to make an X block. Repeat to make four X blocks.

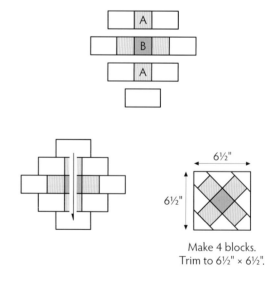

| A |
| B |
| A |

6½"

6½"

Make 4 blocks.
Trim to 6½" × 6½".

4 Matching the seams of the segments as shown and rotating every other segment so seams nest, sew together two white 2½" × 4½" rectangles, two A segments, and six B segments in diagonal rows. Centering the red-and-white dot squares, trim

the width of the joined strips to 6½". Then trim the length to 21½" to complete a short X unit. Repeat to make four short X units.

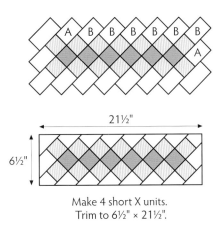

Make 4 short X units.
Trim to 6½" × 21½".

5 Matching the seams of the segments and rotating every other segment so seams nest, join two white 2½" × 4½" rectangles, two A segments, and 16 B segments in diagonal rows. Centering the red-and-white dot squares, trim the width of the joined strips to 6½". Trim the length to 50⅜". Repeat to make four long X units.

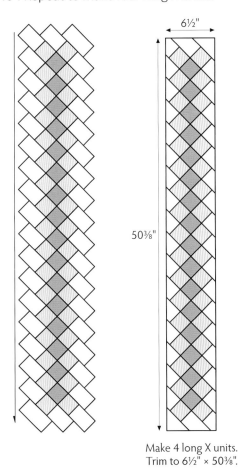

Make 4 long X units.
Trim to 6½" × 50⅜".

Assembling the Quilt Top

1 Referring to the diagram below, lay out the four red 2" × 36½" strips, four X blocks, four short X units, four red 2" × 6½" rectangles, the two red 2" × 21½" strips, and the quilt center in seven vertical rows. Sew together the pieces in each row, and then join the vertical rows. Add the red 2" × 39½" strips to the top and bottom edges. The quilt top should now measure 39½" square, including seam allowances.

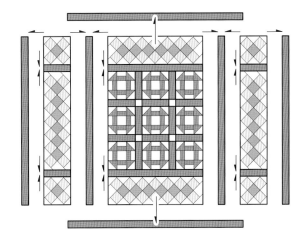

2 Lay out four Churn Dash blocks, six red 2" × 6½" rectangles, one red 2" × 9½" strip, and one red 2" × 24½" strip as shown. Sew together the pieces in each block row, and then sew together each block row with its adjacent sashing strip. Add white side triangles to each end of the rows, and then join the rows. Add a white corner triangle to the top edge to complete a corner unit. Press. Repeat to make four corner units.

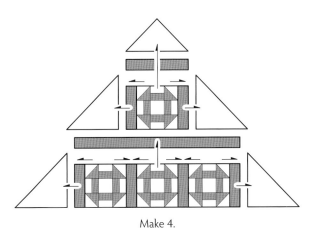

Make 4.

3 Sew the corner units to two opposite edges of the quilt top, and then add corner units to the remaining edges. The quilt top should now measure 55⅝" square, including seam allowances.

Quilt assembly

Adding the Borders

1 Join the remaining red 2"-wide strips end to end and press the seam allowances open. Trim the pieced length into two 58⅝"-long inner-border strips and two 55⅝"-long inner-border strips. Set aside the remainder of the pieced length for the outer border. Sew the shorter strips to the sides of the quilt top, and then add the longer strips to the top and bottom edges. The quilt top should now measure 58⅝" square, including seam allowances.

2 Sew together two white 4⅝" × 6½" rectangles and one long X unit to make a top middle-border strip. Repeat to make a bottom middle-border strip. Each border strip should measure 6½" × 58⅝", including seam allowances.

3 Sew together two white 6½" × 10⅝" rectangles and one long X unit to make a side middle-border strip. Repeat to make a second side middle-border strip. Each border strip should measure 6½" × 70⅝", including seam allowances.

4 Sew the top and bottom middle-border strips to the top and bottom edges of the quilt top, and then add the side middle-border strips. The quilt top should now measure 70⅝" square, including seam allowances.

5 From the remainder of the pieced red 2"-wide strip, trim two 73⅝"-long outer-border strips and two 70⅝"-long outer-border strips. Sew the shorter strips to the sides of the quilt top, and then add the longer strips to the top and bottom edges. The completed quilt top should measure 73⅝" square.

Adding borders

Susan says...

I wanted to make a quilt that looked like a medallion but that wasn't assembled like a typical medallion, in rounds. This faux medallion is way easier to make than it looks. You just sew the blocks into a straight-row unit, and then set that unit on point and surround it with a border of strip-pieced units.

Finishing the Quilt

If you need detailed instructions about any of the finishing steps, go to ShopMartingale.com for free downloadable information.

1 Prepare the quilt backing so it is about 8" larger in both directions than the quilt top.

2 Layer the backing, batting, and quilt top. Baste the layers together.

3 Hand or machine quilt as desired; the quilt shown was quilted with an allover design of fleur-de-lis and feathers.

4 Using the red gingham 2½"-wide bias strips, make the binding and attach it to the quilt.

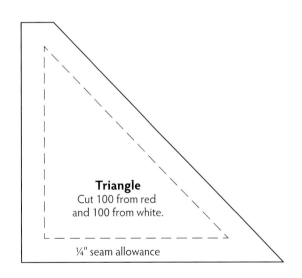

Triangle
Cut 100 from red
and 100 from white.

¼" seam allowance

Train Tracks

The name for this quilt comes from memories of laying train tracks around the Christmas tree. The blocks seemed to take on the shape of the train-track pieces I remember pulling out of the box.

QUILT SIZE: 75" × 90"
BLOCK SIZE: 8½" × 19¾"

Materials

Yardage is based on 42"-wide fabric unless otherwise noted.

62 strips, 2½" × 42", of assorted prints for blocks

5⅔ yards of cream solid for blocks, sashing, border, and binding

7⅝ yards of fabric for backing

83" × 98" piece of batting

Cutting

All measurements include ¼" seam allowances.

From *each* of the 62 assorted print strips, cut:

2 strips, 2½" × 18" (124 total)

1 square, 2½" × 2½" (62 total; 6 will be extra)

From the cream solid, cut:

9 strips, 3½" × 42"

47 strips, 2½" × 42"; crosscut *38 of the strips* into:

◆ 56 strips, 2½" × 18"

◆ 168 squares, 2½" × 2½"

18 strips, 2" × 42"

Making the Blocks

Press the seam allowances as indicated by the arrows.

1. Sew together two cream 2½" × 18" strips and five assorted print 2½" × 18" strips as shown to make strip set A. Repeat to make 20 strip sets. Crosscut each strip set into seven A segments, 2½" wide (140 A segments total).

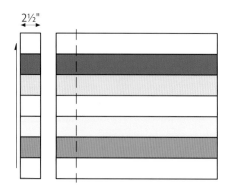

Strip set A. Make 20.
Cut 140 A segments.

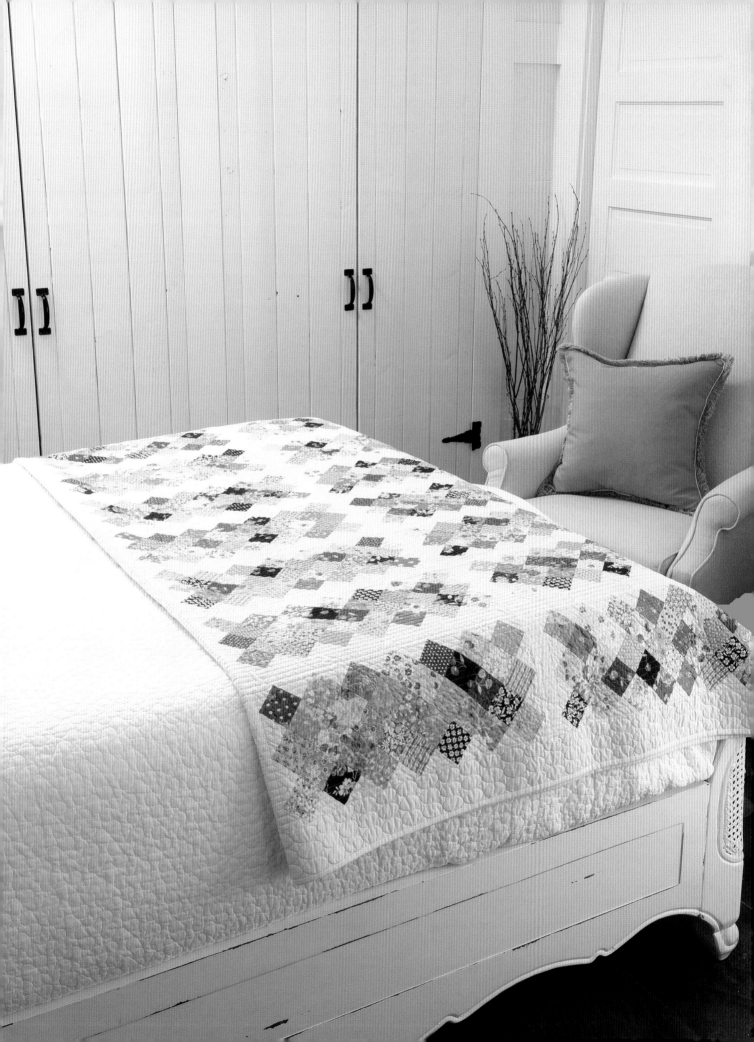

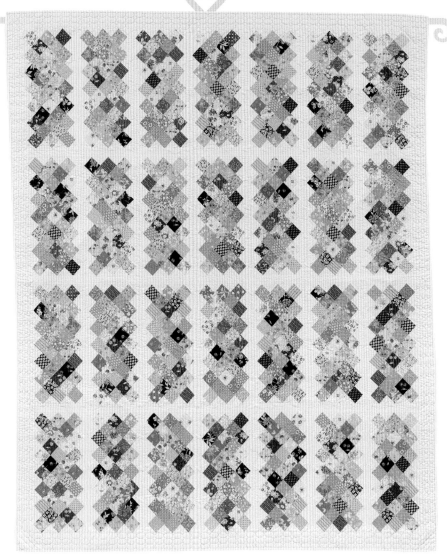

Susan says...

Mix in as many colors as you like and don't worry about their placement. If you start with an equal number of strips of each color (they don't have to be the same print, just the same color), then it's practically like sewing with your eyes closed. The prints will become jumbled up and the result will be a fun, scrappy quilt.

2 Sew together two cream 2½" × 18" strips and three assorted print 2½" × 18" strips as shown to make strip set B. Repeat to make eight strip sets. Crosscut each strip set into seven B segments, 2½" wide (56 B segments total).

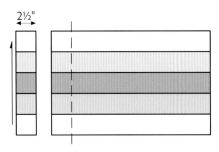

Strip set B. Make 8.
Cut 56 B segments.

3 Sew together two cream 2½" squares and one print 2½" square as shown to make segment C. Repeat to make 56 C segments.

Segment C.
Make 56, 2½" × 6½".

4 Referring to the block assembly diagram, lay out two cream 2½" squares, two C segments, two B segments, and five A segments in diagonal rows. Rotate the segments as needed so that the seam allowances alternate directions. Matching the seams of the segments as shown, sew together

the squares and segments. Trim the edges of each block ¼" from the points of the squares to make a block that measures 9" × 20¼", including seam allowances. Repeat to make 28 blocks.

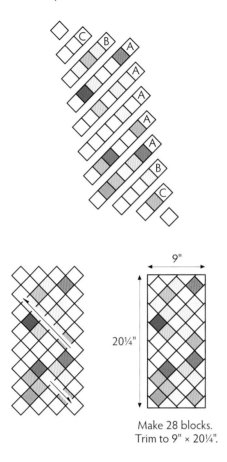

Make 28 blocks.
Trim to 9" × 20¼".

Assembling the Quilt Top

1 Join the cream 2" × 42" strips end to end and press the seam allowances open. Trim the pieced length into three sashing strips, 69" long, and 24 sashing rectangles, 2" × 20¼".

2 Lay out the blocks in four rows of seven blocks each, adding the sashing rectangles and strips as shown in the quilt assembly diagram. Sew

together the pieces in each row, and then join the rows. The quilt top should measure 69" × 84", including seam allowances.

Quilt assembly

3 Join the cream 3½" × 42" strips end to end and press the seam allowances open. Trim the pieced length into two 84"-long border strips and two 75"-long border strips. Sew the longer strips to the sides of the quilt top and press the seam allowances toward the borders. Sew the shorter strips to the top and bottom edges of the quilt top and press the seam allowances toward the borders. The completed quilt top should measure 75" × 90".

Finishing the Quilt

If you need detailed instructions about any of the finishing steps, go to ShopMartingale.com for free downloadable information.

1 Prepare the quilt backing so it is about 8" larger in both directions than the quilt top.

2 Layer the backing, batting, and quilt top. Baste the layers together.

3 Hand or machine quilt as desired; the quilt shown was quilted with vertical lines of stitching.

4 Using the remaining cream 2½"-wide strips, make the binding and attach it to the quilt.

Pumpkin Maze

Easy and fun are rolled into one
with a pumpkin-inspired triple Irish Chain
that's just perfect for fall.

QUILT SIZE: 80½" × 80½"
BLOCK SIZE: 14" × 14"

Materials

Yardage is based on 42"-wide fabric unless otherwise noted.

18 strips, 2½" × 42", of assorted green prints for blocks

36 strips, 2½" × 42", of assorted orange prints for blocks and middle border

12 strips, 2½" × 42", of assorted gray prints for Irish Chain blocks

12 strips, 2½" × 42", of assorted off-white prints for Irish Chain blocks

8 strips, 2½" × 42", of assorted black prints for Irish Chain blocks

2⅔ yards of cream solid for Pumpkin blocks and borders

1 strip, 2½" × 42", of light brown print for Pumpkin blocks

¾ yard of light green solid for binding

7⅝ yards of fabric for backing

89" × 89" piece of batting

Easy Angle tool *OR* template plastic

Cutting

All measurements include ¼" seam allowances. To cut triangles for the half-square-triangle units from 2½"-wide strips, I use the Easy Angle acrylic tool. If you prefer, trace the triangle pattern on page 58 onto template plastic and cut out the shape on the drawn lines. Trace the template onto the wrong side of the 2½"-wide strips specified below, rotating the template 180° after each cut to make the best use of your fabric.

From *each of 12* green print strips, cut:

1 strip, 2½" × 32" (12 total)

From *1* of the green print strips, cut:

12 squares, 2½" × 2½"

From *each of 16* orange print strips, cut:

1 strip, 2½" × 32" (16 total)

2 rectangles, 2½" × 3½" (32 total)

From *each of 4* orange print strips, cut:

5 rectangles, 2½" × 3½" (20 total)

12 triangles using Easy Angle or triangle pattern (48 total)

From *each of 4* orange print strips, cut:

11 rectangles, 2½" × 3½" (44 total)

Continued on page 54

Continued from page 52

From the cream solid, cut:

4 strips, 6½" × 32"

14 strips, 2½" × 42"; crosscut *5 of the strips* into a total of:

- ◆ 12 rectangles, 2½" × 5"
- ◆ 12 rectangles, 2½" × 3"
- ◆ 4 squares, 2½" × 2½"
- ◆ 48 triangles using Easy Angle or triangle pattern

17 strips, 1½" × 42; crosscut *9 of the strips* into a total of 228 squares, 1½" × 1½"

From the light brown print, cut:

12 rectangles, 1½" × 2½"

From the light green solid, cut:

9 strips, 2½" × 42"

Making the Irish Chain Blocks

Press the seam allowances as indicated by the arrows.

1 Sew together two green, two orange, two gray, and one off-white 2½" × 42" strip as shown to make strip set A. Make two. Crosscut the strip sets into 26 A segments, 2½" wide.

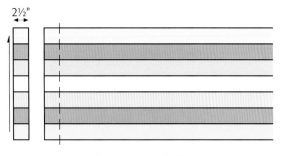

Strip set A. Make 2.
Cut 26 A segments.

2 Sew together two orange, two gray, two off-white, and one black 2½" × 42" strip as shown to make strip set B. Make two. Crosscut the strip sets into 26 B segments, 2½" wide.

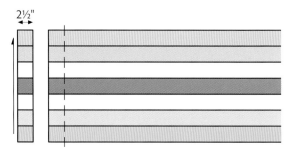

Strip set B. Make 2.
Cut 26 B segments.

3 Sew together two gray, two off-white, two black, and one orange 2½" × 42" strip as shown to make strip set C. Make two. Crosscut the strip sets into 26 C segments, 2½" wide.

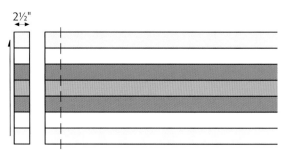

Strip set C. Make 2.
Cut 26 C segments.

4 Sew together two off-white, two black, two orange, and one green 2½" × 42" strip as shown to make strip set D. Crosscut the strip set into 13 D segments, 2½" wide.

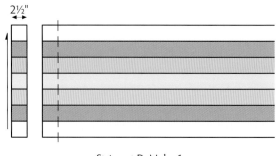

Strip set D. Make 1.
Cut 13 D segments.

5 Join two A segments, two B segments, two C segments, and one D segment to make an Irish Chain block measuring 14½" square, including seam allowances. Make 13 Irish Chain blocks.

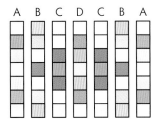 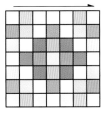

Make 13 blocks,
14½" × 14½".

Making the Pumpkin Blocks

1 Join a cream triangle and an orange triangle to make a half-square-triangle unit. The unit should measure 2½" square, including seam allowances. Make 48 half-square-triangle units.

Make 48,
2½" × 2½".

2 Sew together three assorted orange 2½" × 32" strips to make strip set E. Make two. Crosscut the strip sets into 24 E segments, 2½" wide.

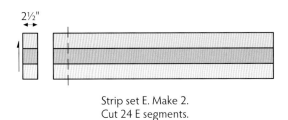

2½"

Strip set E. Make 2.
Cut 24 E segments.

3 Sew together five assorted orange 2½" × 32" strips to make strip set F. Make two. Crosscut the strip sets into 24 F segments, 2½" wide.

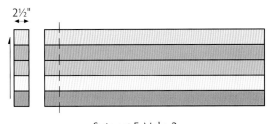

2½"

Strip set F. Make 2.
Cut 24 F segments.

4 Use a pencil to mark a diagonal line on the wrong side of each cream 1½" square.

5 Align a marked square right side down on one end of a light brown 1½" × 2½" rectangle as shown. Sew on the drawn line. Trim the seam allowances to ¼" and press the resulting triangle toward the corner to make a stem unit. Repeat to make 12 stem units.

Stem unit.
Make 12,
1½" × 2½".

6 Using the same stitch-and-flip method as in step 5, add two marked squares to opposite corners of a green 2½" square to make a leaf unit. Repeat to make 12 leaf units. Set aside the remaining marked squares for the middle border.

Leaf unit.
Make 12,
2½" × 2½".

7 Lay out one cream 2½" × 5" rectangle, one stem unit, one leaf unit, one cream 2½" × 3" rectangle, four half-square-triangle units, two of segment E, and two of segment F in five rows as shown. Sew together the pieces in each row, and then join the rows to make a Pumpkin block center. The block center should measure 10½" square, including seam allowances. Repeat to make 12 Pumpkin block centers.

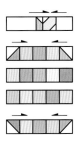

Make 12,
10½" × 10½".

Susan says...

I started this design by coloring in an Irish Chain quilt plan. I had only a few gray strips, so I had to figure out how and where to best use them. Once the color scheme was planned, the rest was easy. This pattern uses mostly 2½"-wide strips, so get ready for some strip-piecing fun.

8 Sew together two green 2½" × 32" strips and one cream 6½" × 32" strip to make strip set G. Press. Make two. Crosscut the strip sets into 24 G segments, 2½" wide.

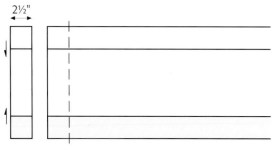

Strip set G. Make 2.
Cut 24 G segments.

9 Sew together four green 2½" × 32" strips and one cream 6½" × 32" strip as shown to make strip set H. Press. Make two. Crosscut the strip sets into 24 H segments, 2½" wide.

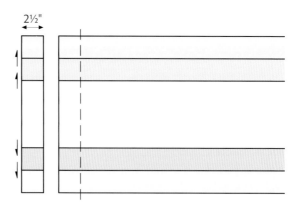

Strip set H. Make 2.
Cut 24 H segments.

10 Sew G segments to the sides of a Pumpkin block center. Add H segments to the top and bottom edges to complete a Pumpkin block. The block should measure 14½" square, including seam allowances. Repeat to make 12 Pumpkin blocks.

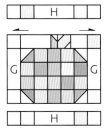 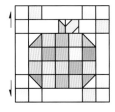

Make 12 blocks,
14½" × 14½".

Assembling the Quilt Top

Referring to the quilt assembly diagram, lay out the Irish Chain blocks and Pumpkin blocks in five rows of five blocks each. Sew together the blocks in each row, and then join the rows. The quilt top should measure 70½" square, including seam allowances.

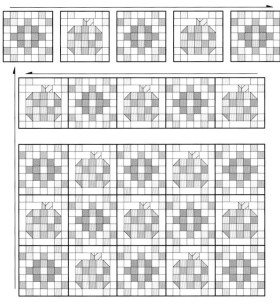

Quilt assembly

Adding the Borders

1 Join the remaining cream 1½" × 42" strips end to end and press the seam allowances open. Trim the pieced length into two 72½"-long inner-border strips and two 70½"-long inner-border strips. Sew the shorter strips to the sides of the quilt top, and then add the longer strips to the top and bottom edges. The quilt top should now measure 72½" square, including seam allowances.

2 Using the same stitch-and-flip method as for the Pumpkin blocks, add two marked cream 1½" squares to an orange 2½" × 3½" rectangle to make a border unit. Make 48 border units. Repeat to make 48 mirror-image border units.

Border unit.
Make 48,
2½" × 3½".

Mirror-image border unit.
Make 48,
2½" × 3½".

3 Sew together 12 border units and 12 mirror-image border units to make a middle-border strip. Repeat to make four strips that measure 2½" × 72½", including seam allowances.

Make 4,
2½" × 72½".

4 Add a cream 2½" square to each end of two strips to make the top and bottom middle borders, which should each measure 2½" × 76½".

Make 2,
2½" × 76½".

5 Sew the middle-border strips without end squares to the sides of the quilt top, and then add the top and bottom middle-border strips. The quilt top should now measure 76½" square, including seam allowances.

6 Join the remaining cream 2½" × 42" strips end to end and press the seam allowances open. Trim the pieced length into two 80½"-long outer-border strips and two 76½"-long outer-border strips. Sew the shorter strips to the sides of the quilt top, and then add the longer strips to the top and bottom edges. The completed quilt top should measure 80½" square.

Finishing the Quilt

If you need detailed instructions about any of the finishing steps, go to ShopMartingale.com for free downloadable information.

1 Prepare the quilt backing so it is about 8" larger in both directions than the quilt top.

2 Layer the backing, batting, and quilt top. Baste the layers together.

3 Hand or machine quilt as desired; the quilt shown was quilted with an overall spiderweb design.

4 Using the light green 2½"-wide strips, make the binding and attach it to the quilt.

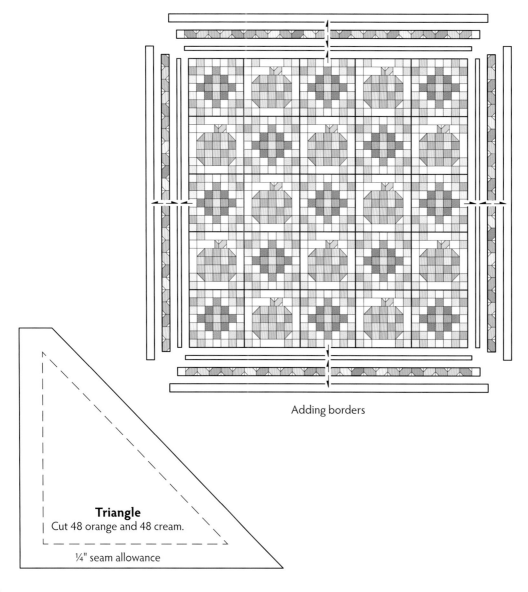

Adding borders

Triangle
Cut 48 orange and 48 cream.

¼" seam allowance

Double Date

Using the softest of soft seaside colors, I set out to create something that was sweet enough for a baby quilt but that could also do double duty as a great table topper.

QUILT SIZE: 52½" × 52½"
BLOCK SIZE: 6" × 6"

Materials

Yardage is based on 42"-wide fabric unless otherwise noted.

2 strips, 2½" × 42", *each of 9* assorted solids for blocks and sashing squares

3 yards of cream solid for blocks, sashing, border, and binding

3⅜ yards of fabric for backing

59" × 59" piece of batting

Tri-Recs and Easy Angle tools *OR* template plastic

Cutting

All measurements include ¼" seam allowances. To cut triangles for star-point units and half-square-triangle units from 2½"-wide strips, I use the Tri-Recs and Easy Angle acrylic tools. If you prefer, trace triangle patterns A, B, and C on page 63 onto template plastic and cut out the shapes on the drawn lines. Trace the templates onto the wrong side of the 2½"-wide strips specified below, rotating the templates 180° after each cut to make the best use of your fabric.

From *each* of the 9 assorted solids, cut:

7 squares, 2½" × 2½" (63 total; 2 will be extra)

16 B triangles using Recs tool or triangle B pattern (144 total)

16 B reversed triangles using Recs tool or triangle B pattern reversed (144 total)

12 C triangles using Easy Angle or triangle C pattern (108 total; 8 will be extra)

From the cream solid, cut:

6 strips, 3½" × 42"

31 strips, 2½" × 42"; crosscut *25 of the strips* into:

   ◆ 60 rectangles, 2½" × 6½"

   ◆ 44 squares, 2½" × 2½"

   ◆ 144 A triangles using Tri tool or triangle A pattern

   ◆ 100 C triangles using Easy Angle or triangle C pattern

Making the Units

Press the seam allowances as indicated by the arrows.

1 Sew a solid-color B triangle to one edge of a cream A triangle; be sure the blunt tip of the A triangle is pointing down. Add a matching solid-color B reversed triangle to the adjacent edge of the cream triangle as shown to make a star-point unit. The star-point unit should measure 2½" square, including seam allowances. Repeat to make 144 star-point units.

Make 144
star-point units,
2½" × 2½".

2 Sew together a solid-color C triangle and a cream C triangle to make a half-square-triangle unit. The unit should measure 2½" square, including seam allowances. Repeat to make 100 half-square-triangle units (25 sets of 4 matching units).

Make 100,
2½" × 2½".

Assembling the Quilt Top

1 Working on a design wall if possible and referring to the quilt assembly diagram, lay out the star-point units in matching sets of four with a matching solid-color 2½" square to form 36 stars, leaving space between the stars for sashing.

2 To create the effect of Shoofly blocks in the sashing, lay out four matching half-square-triangle units with a matching solid-color 2½" square at each intersection of four stars.

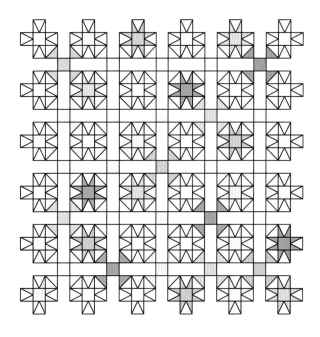

3 Referring to the quilt photo on page 63 if needed, fill in the remaining sashing spaces with cream 2½" × 6½" rectangles and cream 2½" squares.

4 Gather pieces for one Star block. Sew the pieces together in each row, and then join the rows to complete the block. Return the Star block to its place on your design wall. Repeat to make 36 Star blocks that measure 6½" square, including seam allowances.

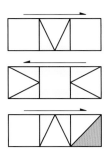 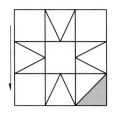

Make 36 blocks,
6½" × 6½".

5 Sew together the blocks, sashing rectangles, and sashing squares in each row, and then join the rows. The quilt top should now measure 46½" square, including seam allowances.

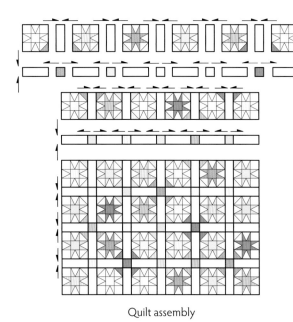

Quilt assembly

6 Join the cream 3½" × 42" strips end to end and press the seam allowances open. Trim the pieced length into two 52½"-long border strips and two 46½"-long border strips. Sew the shorter strips to the sides of the quilt top and press the seam allowances toward the borders. Sew the longer strips to the top and bottom edges and press the seam allowances toward the border. The completed quilt top should measure 52½" square.

Finishing the Quilt

If you need detailed instructions about any of the finishing steps, go to ShopMartingale.com for free downloadable information.

1 Prepare the quilt backing so it is about 6" larger in both directions than the quilt top.

2 Layer the backing, batting, and quilt top. Baste the layers together.

3 Hand or machine quilt as desired; the quilt shown was quilted with an allover feather-and-spiral design.

4 Using the remaining cream 2½"-wide strips, make the binding and attach it to the quilt.

Susan says...

Working with solids may seem intimidating if you're not comfortable choosing your own color palette. You can use one similar to mine, choose your own colors, or base your color selection on those used in your favorite prints. Or just make this quilt from your favorite prints. That works too!

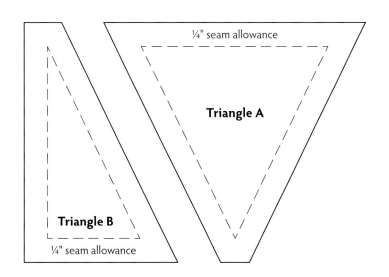

Triangle B

¼" seam allowance

¼" seam allowance

Triangle A

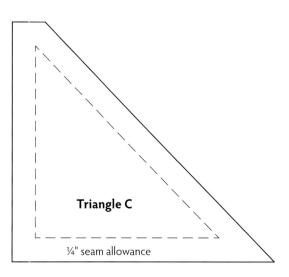

Triangle C

¼" seam allowance

Sea Glass

Usually when I walk on the beach, my head is down so that I can spot
the cool stuff, like sea glass, that washes ashore from the ocean. I knew that
I wanted this quilt to be about soft colors and an overall casual look.

QUILT SIZE: 73½" × 82½"
BLOCK SIZE: 7" × 8"

Materials

Yardage is based on 42"-wide fabric unless otherwise noted.

6⅛ yards of cream solid for blocks, background, borders, and binding

36 strips, 2½" × 42", of assorted medium and dark prints for blocks and outer border

7⅝ yards of fabric for backing

82" × 91" piece of batting

Cutting

All measurements include ¼" seam allowances.

From the cream solid, cut:

8 strips, 8½" × 42"; crosscut into 40 rectangles, 7½" × 8½"

1 strip, 4½" × 42"; crosscut into 4 squares, 4½" × 4½"

45 strips, 2½" × 42"; crosscut *36 of the strips* into 72 strips, 2½" × 21"

8 strips, 1½" × 42"

From the assorted prints, cut a *total* of:

72 strips, 2½" × 21"

Making the Blocks

Press the seam allowances as indicated by the arrows.

1 Sew together one cream and one print 2½" × 21" strip as shown to make a narrow strip set. Make 72 narrow strip sets. From *each* narrow strip set, crosscut four border segments, each 1½" wide (288 total, 10 will be extra); save the remainder of each strip set for the next step.

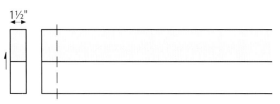

1½"

Make 72 strip sets.
Cut 4 segments from each (288 total).

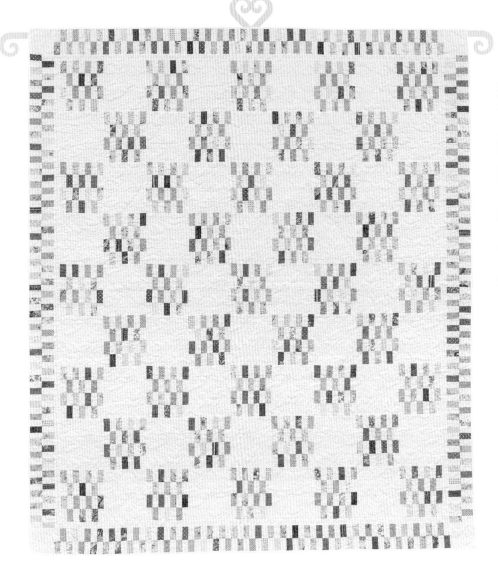

Susan says...

You've probably noticed by now that I love to work with soft, romantic prints. But sometimes they can mush together a bit too much, even for me. To showcase these prints in all their glory, separate them with a creamy solid background and they'll each stand on their own.

2 Sew together two leftover portions of narrow strip sets to make a wide strip set. Make 36 wide strip sets. Crosscut each wide strip set into eight block segments, 1½" wide (288 total).

3 Lay out seven block segments, rotating every other segment as shown. Sew the segments together to make a block that measures 7½" × 8½", including seam allowances. Repeat to make 41 blocks. (You'll have one segment left over.)

1½"

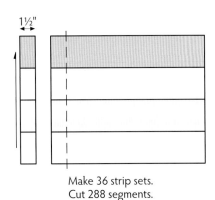

Make 36 strip sets.
Cut 288 segments.

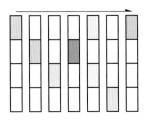

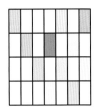

Make 41 blocks,
7½" × 8½".

Assembling the Quilt Top

Lay out the blocks and cream rectangles in nine rows of nine pieces each as shown in the quilt assembly diagram. Sew together the pieces in each row, and then join the rows. The quilt top should measure 63½" × 72½", including seam allowances.

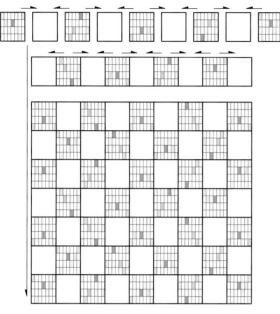

Quilt assembly

Adding the Borders

1 Sew together 74 border segments to make a side outer-border strip. Repeat to make a second strip. These strips should measure 4½" × 74½", including seam allowances.

Make 2 long outer borders
(one is a mirror-image of this),
4½" × 74½".

2 Sew together 65 border segments and two cream 4½" squares to make a top outer-border strip. Repeat to make a bottom outer-border strip. These strips should measure 4½" × 73½", including seam allowances.

Make 2 short outer borders,
4½" × 73½".

3 Join the cream 1½" × 42" strips end to end and press the seam allowances open. Trim the pieced length into two 72½"-long inner-border strips and two 65½"-long inner-border strips. Sew the longer strips to the sides of the quilt top, and then sew the shorter strips to the top and bottom edges.

4 Sew the side outer-border strips to the sides of the quilt top, and then add the top and bottom outer-border strips. The completed quilt top should measure 73½" × 82½".

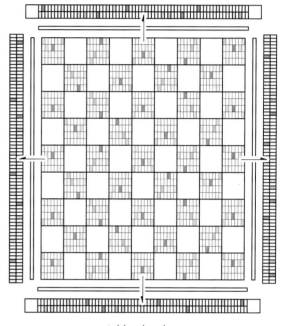

Adding borders

Finishing the Quilt

If you need detailed instructions about any of the finishing steps, go to ShopMartingale.com for free downloadable information.

1 Prepare the quilt backing so it is about 8" larger in both directions than the quilt top.

2 Layer the backing, batting, and quilt top. Baste the layers together.

3 Hand or machine quilt as desired; the quilt shown was quilted with an allover flower-and-dragonfly design.

4 Using the remaining cream 2½"-wide strips, make the binding and attach it to the quilt.

Junkanoo

Junkanoo is the happiest kind of street parade, taking place in the islands of the Bahamas on Boxing Day (December 26) every year. It's loud, it's colorful, and the music is filled with joy. This quilt's pieced stars represent dancing under the nighttime sky, and the scrappy orange and aqua prints perfectly capture the island theme I was after.

QUILT SIZE: 65" × 80"
BLOCK SIZE: 7½" × 7½"

Materials

Yardage is based on 42"-wide fabric unless otherwise noted.

32 squares, 10" × 10", of assorted medium and dark prints for Star blocks

32 squares, 10" × 10", of assorted light prints for Star blocks

13 strips, 2½" × 42", of assorted light prints for Log Cabin blocks and inner border

19 strips, 2½" × 42", of assorted orange prints for Log Cabin blocks and inner border

25 strips, 2½" × 42", of assorted aqua prints for Log Cabin blocks and inner border

⅞ yard of aqua floral for outer border

⅝ yard of orange floral for binding

5 yards of fabric for backing

73" × 88" piece of batting

Tri-Recs and Easy Angle tools *OR* template plastic

Cutting

All measurements include ¼" seam allowances. To cut triangles for star-point units and half-square-triangle units from 3"-wide strips, I use the Tri-Recs and Easy Angle acrylic tools. If you prefer, trace triangle patterns A, B, and C on page 73 onto template plastic and cut out the shapes on the drawn lines. Trace the templates onto the wrong side of the 3"-wide strips specified below, rotating the templates 180° after each cut to make the best use of your fabric.

From *each* of the 32 medium or dark print squares, cut:

3 strips, 3" × 10"; crosscut into:

- 1 square, 3" × 3" (32 total)

- 4 B triangles using Recs tool or triangle B pattern (128 total)

- 4 B reversed triangles using Recs tool or triangle B pattern reversed (128 total)

- 4 C triangles using Easy Angle or triangle C pattern (128 total)

Continued on page 70

Continued from page 68

From *each* of the 32 light print squares, cut:

3 strips, 3" × 10"; crosscut into:

> 4 A triangles using Tri tool or triangle A pattern (128 total)

> 4 C triangles using Easy Angle or triangle C pattern (128 total)

From *each* of the 13 light print strips, cut:

2 strips, 1¼" × 33"; crosscut into 50 squares, 1¼" × 1¼" (650 total; 10 will be extra)

3 squares, 2" × 2" (39 total)

From the orange print strips, cut a *total* of:

38 strips, 1¼" × 42"; crosscut into:

- ◆ 80 strips, 1¼" × 6½" (D)
- ◆ 80 strips, 1¼" × 5" (C)
- ◆ 80 strips, 1¼" × 3½" (B)
- ◆ 80 strips, 1¼" × 2" (A)

From the aqua print strips, cut a *total* of:

49 strips, 1¼" × 42"; crosscut into:

- ◆ 14 strips, 1¼" × 12½" (H)
- ◆ 14 strips, 1¼" × 11" (G)
- ◆ 14 strips, 1¼" × 9½" (F)
- ◆ 14 strips, 1¼" × 8" (E)
- ◆ 62 strips, 1¼" × 6½" (D)
- ◆ 4 strips, 1¼" × 5¾" (L)
- ◆ 66 strips, 1¼" × 5" (C)
- ◆ 4 strips, 1¼" × 4¼" (K)
- ◆ 66 strips, 1¼" × 3½" (B)
- ◆ 4 strips, 1¼" × 2¾" (J)
- ◆ 66 strips, 1¼" × 2" (A)
- ◆ 4 squares, 1¼" × 1¼" (I)

From the aqua floral, cut:

8 strips, 3½" × 42"

From the orange floral, cut:

8 strips, 2½" × 42"

Making the Star Blocks

Press the seam allowances as indicated by the arrows.

1 Sew a medium or dark B triangle to one edge of a light A triangle; be sure the blunt tip of the A triangle is pointing down. Add a matching medium or dark B reversed triangle to the adjacent edge of the cream triangle as shown to make a star-point unit. The star-point unit should measure 3" square, including seam allowances. Repeat to make four matching star-point units.

Make 4
star-point units,
3" × 3".

2 Using the same prints as in step 1, sew together a medium or dark C triangle and a light C triangle to make a half-square-triangle unit. The unit should measure 3" square. Repeat to make four matching half-square-triangle units.

Make 4,
3" × 3".

3 Lay out the half-square-triangle units, star-point units, and the matching medium or dark 3" square in three rows as shown. Sew together the pieces in each row, and then join the rows to make a Star block that measures 8" square, including seam allowances. Make 32 Star blocks.

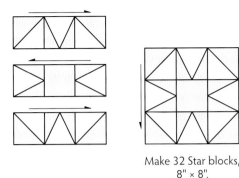

Make 32 Star blocks, 8" × 8".

Making the Log Cabin Blocks

1 Sew a light 1¼" square to each end of the orange A, B, C, and D strips.

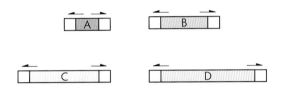

2 Sew aqua A strips to the top and bottom edges of a light 2" square. Sew pieced orange A strips to the side edges. Working alphabetically, continue to add aqua and then pieced orange B, C, and D strips to make a Log Cabin block. Press all seam allowances toward the just-added strip. Repeat to make 31 Log Cabin blocks that measure 8" square, including seam allowances. You will use the remaining pieced strips in the inner border.

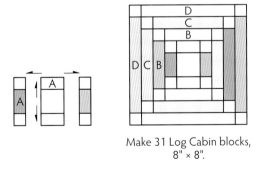

Make 31 Log Cabin blocks, 8" × 8".

Assembling the Quilt Top

Referring to the quilt assembly diagram, lay out the Star blocks and Log Cabin blocks in nine rows of seven blocks each. Sew the blocks in each row together, and then join the rows. The quilt top

should now measure 53" × 68", including seam allowances.

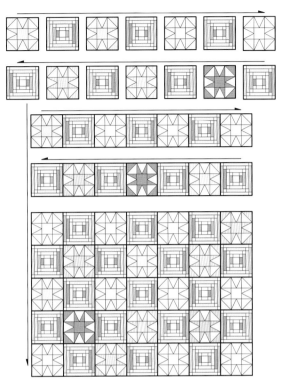

Quilt assembly

Adding the Borders

1 To make the side inner borders, lay out five each of pieced orange A, B, C, and D strips; four each of aqua E, F, G, and H strips; two each of aqua A and J strips; and two aqua I squares in four rows as shown. Join the pieces in each row. Press all seam allowances toward the aqua pieces. Join the rows to make a side inner border. Press the seam allowances in one direction. The pieced border should measure 3½" × 68", including seam allowances. Repeat to make a second side inner border.

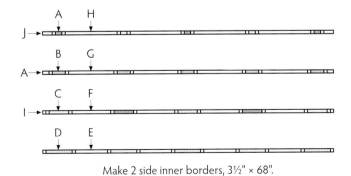

Make 2 side inner borders, 3½" × 68".

Susan says...

I didn't strip piece this quilt at all, because I had a limited number of orange and aqua fabrics. Instead, I cut and then chain pieced so that I could easily move the colors around until I was completely pleased with the layout.

2   For the top inner border, lay out four each of pieced orange A, B, C, and D strips; three each of aqua E, F, G, and H strips; and two each of aqua B, C, K, and L strips in four rows as shown at right. Sew together the pieces in each row. Press all seam allowances toward the aqua pieces. Join the rows to make the top inner border. Press the seam allowances in one direction. The pieced border should measure 3½" × 59", including seam allowances. Repeat to make the bottom inner border.

3   Sew the side inner borders to the sides of the quilt top, and then add the top and bottom inner borders. The quilt top should now measure 59" × 74", including seam allowances.

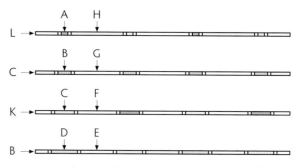

Make 2 top/bottom inner borders, 3½" × 59".

4 Join the aqua floral 3½" × 42" strips end to end and press the seam allowances open. Trim the pieced length into two 74"-long outer-border strips and two 65"-long outer-border strips. Sew the longer strips to the sides of the quilt top, and then add the shorter strips to the top and bottom edges. The completed quilt top should measure 65" × 80".

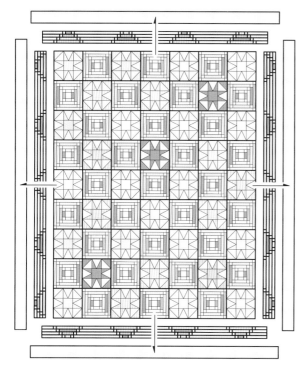

Adding borders

Finishing the Quilt

If you need detailed instructions about any of the finishing steps, go to ShopMartingale.com for free downloadable information.

1 Prepare the quilt backing so it is about 8" larger in both directions than the quilt top.

2 Layer the backing, batting, and quilt top. Baste the layers together.

3 Hand or machine quilt as desired; the quilt shown was quilted with an allover floral design.

4 Using the orange floral 2½"-wide strips, make the binding and attach it to the quilt.

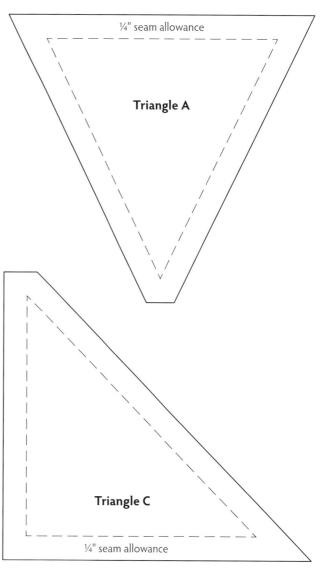

¼" seam allowance

Triangle A

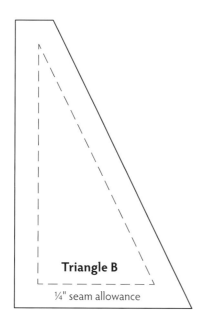

Triangle B

¼" seam allowance

Triangle C

¼" seam allowance

The Guest Room

This is the quilt that I would want in a guest room—something that looks delightfully soft and old, as if it had been passed down from a family member. That is why I named it The Guest Room.

QUILT SIZE: 67¼" × 82½"
BLOCK SIZE: 13" × 13"

Materials

Yardage is based on 42"-wide fabric unless otherwise noted.

50 strips, 2½" × 42", of assorted light, medium, and dark prints for Dresden wedges

4¼ yards of white solid for block backgrounds and sashing squares

4 yards of pink gingham for quarter-circle appliqués, sashing strips, border, and binding

5⅛ yards of fabric for backing

76" × 91" piece of batting

Freezer paper

Easy Dresden tool *OR* template plastic

Cutting

All measurements include ¼" seam allowances. To cut wedges for the blocks from 2½"-wide strips, I use the Easy Dresden acrylic tool. If you prefer, trace the wedge pattern on page 79 onto template plastic and cut out the shape on the drawn lines. Trace the template onto the wrong side of the 2½" × 5" rectangles specified below to make the required number of wedges.

From *each* of the 50 light, medium, and dark print strips, cut:

8 rectangles, 2½" × 5"; cut each rectangle into a wedge using Easy Dresden or wedge pattern (400 total)

From the white solid, cut:

10 strips, 13½" × 42"; crosscut into 20 squares, 13½" × 13½"

1 strip, 2¾" × 42"; crosscut into 12 squares, 2¾" × 2¾"

From the pink gingham, cut:

8 strips, 4½" × 42"

16 strips, 2¾" × 42"; crosscut into 31 strips, 2¾" × 13½"

Enough 2½"-wide bias strips to total 315" in length for binding

Susan says...

You have to love making Dresden Plate blocks to undertake this quilt. But let's be serious. Who wouldn't want to sleep under this beauty in your guest room? When your guests ooh and ahh over this quilt, you'll know it was worth the effort.

Preparing the Appliqués

Press the seam allowances as indicated by the arrows.

1 Using the circle pattern on page 79, trace the shape 20 times onto the dull side of freezer paper. Cut out the freezer-paper circles on the drawn lines.

2 Using a hot, dry iron, press each freezer-paper circle onto the wrong side of the remaining pink gingham, leaving ½" between circles. Cut out each fabric circle, adding ¼" seam allowance beyond the freezer paper.

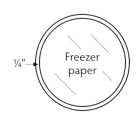

¼" Freezer paper

3 Using the tip of your iron, press the seam allowance over the edge of each freezer-paper circle to the wrong side.

4 Cut a prepared circle in half horizontally and vertically to make four quarter-circle appliqués. Repeat to make 80 quarter-circle appliqués.

Make 80.

5 Fold a fabric wedge in half lengthwise with the long edges together. On the wide end of the folded piece, sew the ends together with a ¼" seam allowance. Turn the piece right side out and press flat, creating a point at the end of the wedge. Repeat to prepare all 400 wedges.

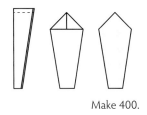

Make 400.

Susan says...

Many of my favorite color combinations are a result of *not* planning them. When making a scrappy quilt, you will run across colors side by side that you may never have dreamed of before. Lay out your colors, walk away, and come back later. If you return and still love what's in front of you, you'll probably love them in your quilt. I call this part of my process "simmering." It lets me decide if my overall desired look is being achieved, and it's the best time to edit blocks and colors.

6 Select five assorted wedges and sew them together along the raw edges to make a quarter Dresden unit. Repeat to make 12 sets of four matching quarter Dresden units. Also make 14 pairs of matching quarter Dresden units.

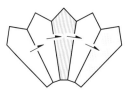

Quarter Dresden unit.
Make 76.

7 Select two pairs of matching wedges and one additional wedge. Sew the pieces together as shown. Repeat to make four corner Dresden units.

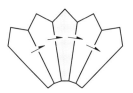

Corner quarter Dresden unit.
Make 4.

and baste the raw edges together if desired. Return the block to its place on your design wall. Repeat to make 20 blocks.

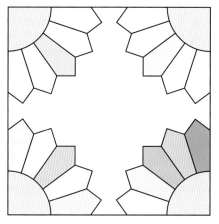

Make 20 blocks,
13½" × 13½".

Assembling the Quilt Top

1 Referring to the quilt assembly diagram below right and the quilt photo on page 76, lay out the white 13½" and 2¾" squares and pink 2¾" × 13½" rectangles in nine horizontal rows. At each intersection of four blocks, position a matching quarter Dresden unit in the corner of each white background square. Position the four corner Dresden units on the white background squares in the four outer corners of the quilt. Then fill in each open side edge of the white background squares with pairs of matching quarter Dresden units.

2 Pick up the first background square and its four quarter Dresden units. Pin or glue baste the Dresden units in place, matching the raw edges. Position a pink quarter-circle appliqué in each corner of the background square, covering the raw edges of the Dresden units; pin or glue baste. Using a narrow zigzag or blanket stitch and monofilament, stitch along the turned-under edge of each Dresden unit and quarter-circle appliqué to make a block. Remove the freezer paper from the appliqué shapes

3 Sew together the blocks and sashing pieces in each row, and then join the rows. The quilt top should now measure 59¼" × 74½", including seam allowances.

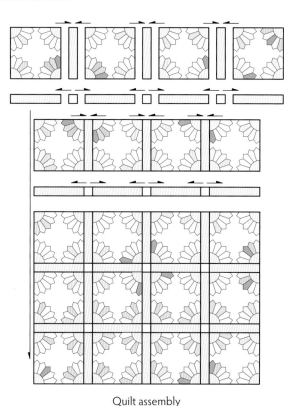

Quilt assembly

4 Join the pink 4½" × 42" strips end to end and press the seam allowances open. Trim the pieced length into two 74½"-long border strips and two 67¼"-long border strips. Sew the longer strips to the side edges of the quilt top and press the seam allowances toward the borders. Sew the shorter strips to the top and bottom edges and press the seam allowances toward the borders. The completed quilt top should measure 67¼" × 82½".

Finishing the Quilt

If you need detailed instructions about any of the finishing steps, go to ShopMartingale.com for free downloadable information.

1 Prepare the quilt backing so it is about 8" larger in both directions than the quilt top.

2 Layer the backing, batting, and quilt top. Baste the layers together.

3 Hand or machine quilt as desired; the quilt shown was quilted with an allover feather-and-spiral design.

4 Using the pink gingham 2½"-wide bias strips, make the binding and attach it to the quilt.

¼" seam allowance

Wedge
Cut 8 each from
each print strip.

Circle
Cut 20 from
freezer paper.

About the Author

Acknowledgments

It's taken a lot of steps to get to this moment of actually seeing my name in print on a quilt book, so there are many people I'd like to thank (and hug!).

I'm lucky to have a crazy, loving, and supportive **family** that's always willing to endure my endless questions about color and layout and builds me up when I question my quilting abilities. Thank you for hanging in there with me and always being ready with reassuring words.

Thanks to **Susan Rogers** for adding that magic long-arm quilting touch. Without you, Susan, these quilts would just be pieces of fabric sewn together. Thank you for your creative touch that makes my quilt tops burst to life.

Lissa Alexander, there will always be a place in my heart for you and your never-ending kindness. You have steered me in directions I would have never thought possible. I can't thank you enough for taking an interest in me.

Thanks to **Moda Fabrics.** Beyond the gorgeous fabric that you produce and the brilliant designers who bring daily color to my life, you've also been in my corner every step of my creative journey.

I will forever be grateful for **Lisa Christensen's** ability to help put together quilt layouts by reading scribbles of measurements on sticky notes.

Elizabeth Beese, thank you for your endless patience and undeniable professionalism each and every step of the way. Your abilities as a technical editor are such a gift, and I'll always be your number-one fan.

Thank you to my **social-media friends.** I promise that this book would not have been written had it not been for you watching and commenting on my frequent pictures on Instagram. Thank you for following @yardgrl60 and playing along with my love of fabric and fibers.

Finally, thank you **Martingale:** many quilting friendships have been made through this book process. This has been the best experience ever for my quilting passion. Thank you for believing that a book of my patterns would be welcome in the quilting industry.

Susan Ache

Knowing only that she wanted to feature embroidery and Nine Patch blocks, Susan Ache taught herself to make her first quilt. Quiltmaking opened up a new world to this mom of five now-grown children. She turned many hours reading about quiltmaking into a lifelong passion for creating beautiful quilts.

Susan finds color inspiration in her native Florida surroundings. She's always searching for new and fun ways to show off as many colors as she can in a quilt. Most of her quilts are a creative impulse inspired by a trip to the garden center, a photograph in a magazine, or a few paint color swatches. She never sees just the quilt—she sees the room where the quilt belongs.

Working in a quilt store for years helped cultivate Susan's love of color and fabric. Visit Susan on Pinterest and Instagram as @yardgrl60.

What's your creative passion?

Find it at **ShopMartingale.com**

books • eBooks • ePatterns • blog • free projects
videos • tutorials • inspiration • giveaways

Martingale
Create with Confidence